# The Dispatch Carrier

# The Dispatch Carrier

A Sergeant of the 9th Illinois Cavalry, Union
Army on Campaign and in Andersonville Prison
During the American Civil War

Wm. N. Tyler

LEONAUR

*The Dispatch Carrier*
*A Sergeant of the 9th Illinois Cavalry, Union Army on Campaign and*
*in Andersonville Prison During the American Civil War*
by Wm. N. Tyler

First published under the title
*The Dispatch Carrier and Memoirs of Andersonville Prison*

Leonaur is an imprint of Oakpast Ltd

Copyright in this form © 2011 Oakpast Ltd

ISBN: 978-0-85706-669-5 (hardcover)
ISBN: 978-0-85706-670-1 (softcover)

http://www.leonaur.com

Publisher's Notes

# Contents

| | |
|---|---|
| Preface | 7 |
| I Join the Union Cavalry | 9 |
| Charging & Foraging | 15 |
| Jim, the Bridge & the Horse | 21 |
| Selected for Dispatch Rider | 28 |
| A Very Close Call | 35 |
| The Government Horses | 41 |
| Gunboats, Bushwackers and Johnnies | 49 |
| Cavalry Sergeant to Infantryman | 57 |
| Battle & Capture | 64 |
| Busting Out | 69 |
| Prison Hell | 78 |
| A Battle to Live | 85 |
| Home | 96 |

# Preface

Books, as a general rule, have prefaces. I write a preface to this book, not because I think it necessary, but because it is customary. I did not keep a diary, and it may be that I have not given the right date every time, but there is nothing in this book but what is strictly true, and the most of it is my own personal experience and that of my comrades who participated in my adventures while a soldier. The reason I do not give the names of my comrades is because they are scattered to the four quarters of the globe, and I do not know where they are except a few who live neighbours to me, and I have no right to use their names without their consent.

I will give a thrilling description of my experience as a dispatch carrier and finally my capture and imprisonment, escape and recapture, and will also give a complete description of being chased by bloodhounds and other incidents too numerous to mention.

Yours Truly,
The Author.

Rapids City, Ills., 1892.

# I Join the Union Cavalry

At the outbreak of the Great Civil War in 1861, I was 23 years of age, a stout, healthy young man, not knowing what it was to have a sick day; had always worked on a farm and worked hard, too. In the latter part of April, news was received that Fort Sumter had been fired upon; everybody acted as if they were crazy; all wanted to enlist. I was one of the first to enlist in a three months' regiment, but that failed to go on account of not having arms, so I was forced to go back to my home, which was four miles south of Belvidere, Ill. In September, 1861, they started to get up a company of cavalry at Belvidere. I was one of the first to enlist in that, after which I was appointed sergeant. We were sent to Camp Douglas, Chicago.

It did not take long to fill up our regiment, neither did it take long to get our horses and saddles ready; then we commenced to drill. What a time some of our men had; some had never driven a horse in their lives and there is where the fun comes in, especially after we had drawn our spurs. The next move after we had drawn our spurs and saddles was when Colonel Brackett ordered the bugle to sound the call to fall in for drill. The whole regiment was on hand with their horses all saddled and bridled for a drill. You must remember that our horses were well fed and in the best condition; full of life and spirt. It was all some of us could do to make them keep their place in the ranks.

"Now," said the colonel, "When I tell you to mount you must put your left foot in the stirrup and grasp the reins and the mane with your left hand, and at the word 'mount,' all mount together."

"Mount" was the command. Well, we did make the effort to all mount together but you should have seen them; the horses started off in every direction, pell-mell over the field; some were dragged along on the ground with their feet in the stirrups, while others were on their horses all right, but the harder the horses ran, the harder they stuck in their spurs; one poor fellow let go all hold and grabbed the head and mane; stirrups flew in every direction and he went straight for the barn. Now our stables were all three hundred feet long; away went horse and rider, straight for the centre of the barn; just as the horse got within four feet of the stable, it came to a sudden halt, but the rider went on with a crash through the side of the barn; he could not have made a cleaner hole if he had been shot out of a cannon.

I must say he came out pretty lucky; of course he was bruised and stiff legged for a day or two but that was all. Some of the men got hurt very severely but it did not take long for us to find out that we had to keep our toes in and our heels out. We had not drawn any arms yet and all we had to mount guard with was simply a stick whittled out in shape of a sword. Our officers would not allow any one out unless they had a pass from the colonel. The guards were placed around the camp to keep the men from going out but many nights did the boys run the guard.

If by chance one of the men was out after sundown, the guard was supposed to keep him out or arrest him and turn him over to the sergeant of the guard, but this was generally the way it was done around Camp Douglas: Now, here comes someone who has stayed out after roll call; he comes straight up to the sentinel; the sentinel speaks first: "Who comes there?" now if the man has been out on permission, of course he has the countersign; then he will answer back "A friend with the countersign," then the sentinel wall say, "Advance, friend, and give the countersign," and after giving it the sentinel then passes him in, but let me tell you, we did not always go according to discipline while we were at Chicago. This is the way we had among ourselves: Now here comes one who has been out too late.

"Halt! who comes there?"

"A friend with a canteen."

"Advance and draw the stopple."

The next thing you will see the sentinel look toward heaven, and hear a gurgling sound as of something going down his throat, then finally a pair of lips would smack.

"The countersign is correct, you may pass in."

We had a great many ways of amusing ourselves, some played cards, some football, some one thing and some another, but after all the time hung heavy on our hands for we were all anxious to get into active service. The first of February, 1862, we got marching orders for St. Louis, Mo. Our officers then gave us passes to go home, it being our last chance before leaving for the field. I never shall forget that last visit: how my old mother, wife, and two little ones followed me to the train, how my blessed old mother put her arms around my neck and while the tears were running down those old wrinkled cheeks, called on God to bless her boy.

Oh, that parting! how can we forget it, comrades? to pick up the little ones and give them one long last hug, goodbye, wife, little ones, mother, and we were gone: yes, gone. The next thing was the shrill scream of the engine and we commenced to move slowly out of the depot. The train was mostly loaded with soldiers, all leaving homes, going to fight for their country. There was no screaming or yelling, for they had just parted from their wives, mothers and homes, perhaps never to see them again.

Now just look over the coach of young soldiers in the first flush of manhood; can they all get back to their homes? No, reader, not three out of five.

On we went, every one of those young soldiers knew what they were going for; one could see by their sober, determined faces that they had weighed their chances and had given all for their country.

When we arrived at Chicago, we found everything in a great

state of excitement. We were to embark our horses, equipments, and board the train for St. Louis. All was hurly burly; we had to blindfold our horses in order to get them on the train; finally, all was ready and away we went for St. Louis.

On the 16th of February, 1862, we started for Benton Barracks. At Alton, Ill., we boarded a steamboat for St. Louis; after arriving there we saddled our horses and took them off on the levee, mounted, and commenced our march through the city for Benton Barracks. The streets were lined with people and as the flag bearer unfurled our regimental flag, and as it floated out on the breeze, you could plainly read in large gold letters, "Ninth Illinois Cavalry." We could hear on every side, "What a splendid regiment!" I think I have every reason for being proud of my regiment; all were fine looking young men, fine horses, and as fine a colonel as ever drew a saber. Colonel Brackett was as true and brave an officer as ever wore soldier straps, as the reader will find out if he follows the pages of this true narrative.

As we marched through the streets of St. Louis some hurrahed for the Ninth Illinois Cavalry, while others cursed us to our faces and some yelled, "You won't sit so straight in those saddles when you get down South; you will find lots there that are only two by six." That meant we would find our graves. We paid no attention to their taunts but kept on up through the streets. While we were on Fourth street a woman thrust her head out of a window in the second storey, and exclaimed, "Hurrah for the Ninth Illinois Cavalry and the girl I left behind me!" That set the boys all in good humour, and we arrived at Benton Barracks without any further adventure worthy of note.

The barracks were somewhat in the shape of a square, only a good deal longer than it was wide. They were built to accommodate about fifty thousand troops. The parade ground covered one hundred acres, and the barracks were all around the parade grounds. I do not know just how many troops were there when we were, but should judge that there were about thirty thousand, all waiting for arms, as we had not drawn any as yet ourselves.

Our stables were just in the rear of our quarters, and about all we had to do was to take care of our horses and drill once a day. Sometimes some of our boys were a little quarrelsome, and if a man wanted to fight it did not take long for him to find someone who would accommodate him. Our officers hardly ever interfered; they said it was better to let them fight it out than to be everlastingly quarrelling, and it proved to be the best in the long run, for after we got into the field there was hardly ever any fighting among our own men.

Well, the 22nd of February came around, Washington's birthday, and there was a grand parade of all the soldiers of Benton Barracks. Every soldier had to fall into line to march through the city of St. Louis. Now, reader, step out of the barracks and take a look up and down the long parade ground; first come the buglers, now the drummer and fifers, then the regimental bands, all playing at once; look at the soldiers coming out of the barracks; the parade ground is blue with them as far as the eye can reach, all taking their positions in the ranks. Bugles are sounding, drums, fifes and bands are playing. Then Colonel Brackett comes up, "Prepare to Mount!"

"Mount!" is the command, and the whole regiment is in saddles.

"March," the regiment is in motion.

Then General Smith comes along in front of our regiment. "Well," said he, "I have seen some very fine looking regiments this morning but I must say that the Ninth Illinois Cavalry takes the cake for fine appearance."

Now, reader, do not blame us if we did straighten up a little more in our saddles and try to look more like soldiers.

Away we went; now look back and see the boys in blue coming; first cavalry and artillery, then infantry, bands playing and flags flying. Oh, what a sight! On we go through the city, which has taken on a holiday garb. Every window is full of flags; every place of business shows the stars and stripes, and taking it altogether it was a beautiful sight. The 23rd of February we drew our sabers and revolvers. We received marching orders for Pilot Knob, Mo., whither we started to the lower end of the city, and camped out on the levee. I shall never forget that night; the first night we had ever camped out. The piercing cold wind from the river with no tents to help break it, chilled us through; no wonder no one slept that night. The next morning we put our horses on the train and started for Pilot Knob.

After arriving we went to camp in and around the place. It was a very mountainous country, one mountain after another as far as you could see. We divided off into squads, and every squad had their cooks appointed; we then came down to government rations, hard tack and pork, and you can bet it was hard tack and no mistake; you could scarcely break it with a hammer. We pitched our tents and went into camp life in dead earnest. The citizens told us that the Johnnies had just vacated the place and everybody was on the lookout the first night for an attack from the enemy.

Out on the picket could be heard shot after shot, it being the first night, it kept the camp in a state of excitement. I do not think there was a rebel within forty miles of us; the pickets simply got frightened at the hogs that were running around through the brush. The hogs felt somewhat ashamed of the excitement, and after the first night, our regiment came right up to time and every soldier did his duty like a man.

# Chapter 2

# Charging & Foraging

Well, we were in the field at last, and when we were not drilling or on duty, we were either writing to our friends, or climbing the mountains to see what there was to be seen. Up on Pilot Knob mountain there runs two tracks for the purpose of running the iron ore from the top of the mountain to the bottom where it was melted. The full cars coming down, drew up the empty ones. The mountain is very steep, fully a mile high. Some of the boys of our company would get in the car at the top of the mountain, and get one or two of them in at the bottom, and then take off the brakes; away they came, while the others that got in at the bottom would shoot up like a sky-rocket. We were doing this one day when the ropes broke.

If we had been shot out of a cannon we could hardly have gone much faster. Some went one way and some another. I looked down the mountain, where there was a large pond and as soon as I got the mud and dirt out of my eyes so I could see, the first thing my eyes rested on was two fellows fishing themselves out of the pond. They got off the easiest of any of us, for they simply got a ducking, while the rest of us were all bruised up. The car that we were in did not go over one hundred feet before it busted into ten thousand pieces. We hobbled back to camp to mend our clothes, and came to the conclusion that if any of the rest of them wanted to ride they were welcome to it, for we had all we wanted.

By this time we had grown somewhat used to camp life;

every soldier found out what was required of him. We soon got orders to march south. We reached Black River after going over lofty mountains and through many small towns. It being about the 15th of March when we struck the river, it was bank full and the ice was running at a very rapid rate. As we came up to the river we stopped for a few moments to arrange our blankets to keep them from getting wet and then we plunged in, with Colonel Brackett taking the lead. "Come on, boys," was his command. We all arrived safely, but somewhat wet; our horses had to swim for about two hundred yards. The stream was about three hundred yards wide at this point. There was a Dutchman with us by the name of Sands. He saw a large cake of ice coming straight to him, and, knowing if his horse was struck it would drown, he slid off behind and grabbed the horse by the tail and came out all right. We came very near losing a number of our horses; they were completely chilled, but by perseverance we finally got them safe to land.

As soon as we were all over three of our companies were ordered to mount. The wind blew cold from the north and of course our clothes were wet clear through, but we were young and did not mind this.

About twenty miles from the place where we crossed was a mill where they ground grain and made flour for the surrounding inhabitants. Now at this mill the rebels were stationed; there were about eight hundred, all armed with double-barrelled shotguns. Away we went and when we got within two miles of the Johnnies' camp we stopped to give our horses a rest, and then on we went like the wind. We soon came in sight of the mill; close to it was a bridge where a rebel guard was walking back and forth, with an old double-barrelled shotgun on his shoulder. He was a good specimen of the southern soldier. He was nearly six feet high. On his head he wore a slouch hat, was dressed in his butternut suit and did not look as if he had been shaved for six weeks. The tobacco juice was running down each side of his cheeks, and as we rode up to him he looked up, shifted his tobacco from one check to the other and said, "Who is you'ns?"

Our captain replied, "We are Yanks. Give up your gun; you are a prisoner now."

"I'll be darned! If that don't beat all." He gave up his gun and was taken back to the rear and placed under guard—the first prisoner the Ninth Illinois Cavalry had captured.

About half a mile from the bridge was an open place in the timber, close to the river, and here the Johnnies were camped. They were just organizing and, of course, did not understand about discipline, consequently did not have any camp guard out. We formed a line of battle and charged right into their camp; some started for the timber, some jumped into the river and undertook to swim, and some few got away, but the most of them were captured . They were just in the act of getting supper; their camp kettles hung over the fires all along the camp. Well, now, let me tell you we were hungry and that supper just came in time, and of course we helped the Johnnies eat it. We captured six hundred prisoners, all their camp equipments, about four hundred double-barrelled shotguns and two hundred old muskets and rifles. We sent word back to camp for wagons and teams to haul what we had captured to camp; for the rebels only had two teams and they were as poor specimens as I ever saw.

The "Ninth" came out victorious, and I tell you we were proud; more than proud, for we had an idea that we could clean out the whole Confederacy, but we soon found out that the Johnnies could fight. We put a heavy guard around our prisoners that night and the next morning marched them back to camp.

This being early in the spring of 1862, of course we had not learned much discipline. We had not been in camp long before the camp-diarrhoea broke out; there were twenty-five or thirty deaths, but no wonder, for all we had to eat was hard-tack, bacon and coffee. Most of the "ninth" was made up of farmers, and they had been in the habit of having plenty of everything good to eat, and of course coming down to hard tack was pretty hard on us.

Our business while camping at this place was to forage for our horses, but to forage for ourselves was strictly forbidden. If our boys came in with chickens they had to give an account of how they got them and if they could make the officers believe they had bought them and paid good hard money, it was all right, but if they found out that the boys had stolen them, they would be severely punished. I remember one man who came in with a few potatoes, and as he could not give a straight account as to how he got them, he was forced to carry a rail that weighed 50 pounds for twenty-four hours; but this was in '62. They were not quite so strict in '63, '64 and '65; but you may depend that while the officers were watching us, we were always on the lookout for them.

One bright morning three companies of our regiment got orders to go on a foraging expedition, and I was one to go and I was very glad of it, for mounting guard and drilling began to grow old and anything new was hailed with delight. "Boots and saddles," was the call that rang out in silver notes from our bugles. Every man was in the saddle in an instant. Finally the major gave the command, "March," and we were in motion. The largest part of the command went in advance of the teams. I being a sergeant in my company, was ordered to take ten men to act as rear guards, and, of course, we were in the rear of the wagons, so we had a good opportunity to do a little foraging on our own hook.

We wound around hills, forded creeks and finally came to a halt, about five miles from camp. The teams were still on the side hill and the main body of the men were in the valley below. Up to our right a short distance from the road was a small log cabin with a number of smaller buildings around it. Said I: "Boys, do you think there is any chance for getting anything to eat up there? Now, if someone will stay here and let me know when the command starts, we will go and see what's up there". The understanding between the soldier and teamster was that if the soldier got anything, and the teamster hid it for him in the wagons and took it to camp, they were to divide equally.

I took two men and up the side hill we went; rode up to the fences that surrounded the buildings and dismounted; one man held the horses while my comrade and I jumped over the fence and went up to the house. We rapped on the door, no answer; rapped again, no answer; pulled on the latch string and the door opened. There was no one there; everything lay in all sorts of confusion; chairs, pots and kettles all over the floor, just as if the people had been frightened away. We found nothing to eat there so we went out to the small buildings; opened one after another, but found them all empty except one, and that one had a large fat calf in it.

Comrade Carlyle grabbed him by the neck, I got him by the tail and down the hill we went. We finally got him to the wagon, tied his feet together, and got him in just as the bugle sounded "boots and saddles." On we went, over hills and through valleys; for about five miles; nothing happened within this time only an occasional blat from our calf. We finally came to a large swamp through which our way led, and we forced one of the natives to pilot us through. Now, dear reader, understand that we were in Arkansas and it was not very thickly settled, so you see we had to go some distance from camp to forage.

Arkansas is almost an unbroken forest; hills and swamps, with no bridges to cross on. Understand that I am speaking of war times. After we got through the swamp we came to a beautiful island and here were two large plantations on which was plenty of corn. It was getting late so we went into camp for the night close to one of the farms. Now there were lots of hogs running around, and let me tell you everybody had fresh pork for supper. Some had chicken, and some turkeys; some had potatoes, and I saw one man that had a piece of corn bread with butter to put on it; let me tell you he was getting too high-toned for a soldier. The major put out a strong guard that night but we were not disturbed. The next morning we loaded our wagons and after doing so, we started for camp. Every little while our calf would give an unearthly blat, and the major would run back to look under the wagon and on both sides; finally he got back to the rear guard, and said he, "Sergeant, I have heard several times something like a calf bawling."

"Well, Major, I'll be darned if I haven't heard it, too." The major gave me one look and went back again.

Now for the benefit of the reader that does not understand our army wagons, I will explain them. They were all covered and we had partitioned the back part of the wagon off to make room for our calf, so when the major came back examining the wagon, all he could see was the front part of it and of course that was all full of corn. To say that he was mystified does not describe it, but when he got back to the front he told the captain that some blasted fool of a soldier could blat like a calf. We got back to camp all right and as we had no place to put our corn we left it in the wagon and when it got dark we moved our hams to our mess tent and butchered our calf the next morning. Everybody had a good breakfast and the major ate some of that calf and asked no questions.

# CHAPTER 3

# Jim, the Bridge & the Horse

We stayed some two or three weeks at this place, then got orders to go further south. We arrived at Jacksonport, on White River, and went in camp again. The inhabitants, I might say the whole surrounding country, were the strongest kind of rebels; the town contained about five hundred inhabitants. Just above the town, probably half a mile, the Black and the White Rivers came together and formed a junction, so the White River was navigable from Jacksonport to the Mississippi, which was 150 miles by river. About five miles back of Jacksonport is a swamp that commences at Black River and runs across the country for fifteen miles and empties into White River below the town, so Jacksonport and quite a strip of country was on an island. The reason I give this place such a thorough description is because some very interesting incidents happened here.

About fifteen miles above Jacksonport is a small town called St. Charles, and in order to reach the place by the wagon road we had to cross an old rickety bridge, which was a good half mile in length. We got most of our forage in and around St. Charles. This part of Arkansas is more level but covered by a dense growth of timber. Our regiment had been thinned out some by sickness. We had about 800 fit for duty. Every morning you would see a long string going to the hospital tent to get their quinine. A great many of our boys when they got sick would give up. They did not find mother, sister or wife; no, they did not find home care, and were exposed to storms with nothing but a thin canvas to protect them. Then the sick soldier had no delicacies such as mother would have prepared him. He would hear nothing but rough words. Of course, the boys that waited on the sick did all they could for them, but at the best it was not home. As I said before, some would get sick and home-sick, too, and that kind of a soldier was almost sure to die. When our boys went out foraging they would always bring back something for the sick comrades.

We had one young man in our regiment whom we called Jim. Now this young man does not live far from me today, (as at time of first publication). The reason I do not give his name in full is because his wife does not wish to draw public attention to their family affairs. This young man Jim was always foraging for the sick boys. He would slip around the guards and be gone two or three days at one time. The next thing you knew someone would say, "Here comes Jim." Sure enough, here he comes loaded down with chickens, hams, sweet potatoes, butter, or anything that one could get in the country.

Of course they would punish him severely, but that made no difference with Jim; as soon as he got loose he would give the guard the slip and away he would go again for something good to eat, which he generally found, and gave his sick comrades the lion's share of it. Jim started out one fine morning and as he got to the bridge told the sergeant of the guard that he had a pass to cross the bridge. He had written it himself, but the guard knew no difference so he let him go and on he went till he came to St. Charles. He rode up to a large plantation house, dismounted and tied his horse. Now, Jim was as fine a specimen of a man as one would wish to see; only eighteen years of age, blue eyes, light curly hair and a smile always on his face. As he went up the walk he saw a young lady sitting out on the porch sewing.

Jim walked up to the porch, took off his hat and made a very polite bow. The young lady looked up, took him in from head to foot, then went on with her sewing, paying no more attention to him. Said Jim, "Look here, sis, have you any sweet potatoes, butter, chickens, or anything good to eat? We have some sick soldiers down at camp and I came out to see if I could buy them something good to eat." Jim did not have a cent in his pocket; his plan was to get whatever he could and skip out. Now, I will give you a description of the young lady. She was also eighteen years of age, black eyes that fairly blazed when angry, and when in a good humour they were soft as a fawn's. She was a regular brunette, line form, rather below medium height and beautiful black hair that reached within four inches of the floor when she was standing. Her name was Virginia La Ford and was called a Creole. The girl looked up at him, her eyes blazing, and said, "No sir; we have nothing to sell to the Yankees."

"You haven't? well, that is all right, I will help myself," said Jim. Away he went. An old coloured woman told him to go down cellar, which he did, and got a roll of butter, sweet potatoes, and some honey, then he went back to where the young lady was and said: "Sis, haven't you got any preserves or any kind, of fruit?"

Said she, "Young man, I think you had better look behind you before you go any further." On looking around, what was his astonishment to sec a whole company of rebels riding up to the front of the house.

"Hide me for God's sake, for they will kill me sure."

"Do you think that I am a fool that I would hide you after you have been robbing me?"

"Hide me, please do, and you will never regret it the longest day you live."

"Well, I will hide you." So she took him away up in the garret and left him there. He crawled around some old rubbish and then lay still as a mouse. In the meantime the Johnnies rode up, took Jim's horse, came in and asked what had become of the Yank. The girl told them that he had skipped out to the woods; and after searching everywhere for him, took his horse and went on. The girl went up and told Jim to come down. "Now," said she, "don't think that I hid you because I thought anything of you or your cause, but I hid you because I did not want your stinking carcass in our yard; and now you go, and don't ever show your face here again."

Jim made as polite a bow as he could, thanked her very kindly, and started for camp. At night he came up to my post and told me all his troubles. We took him in, gave him supper, and the next morning took him back to camp. The colonel soon heard of Jim's mishaps, and began to question him. "I understand you have run the guard and been foraging on your own hook."

"Yes, sir," said Jim, his clear, blue eyes looking straight in the colonel's face.

"Well," said the colonel, "I'll try and keep you in camp after this, and he put a ball and chain on him and kept a strict guard over him. Jim was marched off to the guard camp with a ball and chain fastened to his ankle.

These things may seem cruel to the reader, but let me tell you that if we had no discipline you may depend we would not have any army long. Our boys were punished for the most trifling affairs, and then there were times when they were not, when they actually needed it; but as a general rule our officers sympathized with the soldiers when they went out foraging and were always willing to help eat what they got.

A few days after the irons were taken from Jim I was ordered to go on picket guard to the long bridge; I hadn't been there long when who should come up but Jim, on foot and alone. "Hello, Jim! What brought you out here?"

"My legs," said Jim, "and I want to cross that bridge."

"I have orders to shoot the first man that tries to cross that bridge without the countersign," said I.

"All right," said Jim, and before we hardly knew what he was up to, he was half way over, running like a deer. My first thought was that he was deserting. Of course we fired our guns and ordered "Halt," but away he went and disappeared around the bend of the road. About four o'clock in the afternoon we could hear the faint sound of firing in the distance; it came closer and closer, and around the bend in the road we could see the dust rolling up over the trees and the firing grew more distinct. Of course we were always ready for an attack. We formed a line across the bridge, when all at once a man on horseback came in view. Here he comes right on the bridge. Look! The bridge will go down; see how it sways! On he comes. It is our Jim! He passes us like a flash. Here come the Johnnies. Ready, aim, fire! There goes one Johnnie; he is dragged along the ground by one foot. Ah, he is loose. On comes his horse straight across the bridge. "Give them another volley, boys." *Zip, zip*, went the rebels bullets. Now they turn back; away they go around the bend and disappear."

"Hello, Bill," said one of my comrades, "this is a fine horse of the rebs;" he was as wet as if he had just come out of a river. He had been ridden hard and long. Over on the other side of the bridge and on a little rise of ground, in the middle of the road, lay the rider where his comrades had left him. We walked over to him and found him lying on his face, with his eyes wide open. Dead? Yes; he was shot in the left breast. We moved him out to one side of the road and went back to our post.

Just got back when two companies of the Ninth Illinois Cavalry came riding up. Captain Blackburn said, "We heard you were attacked and came to reinforce you." There was no need of that. Before dark a rebel lieutenant came riding up with a white flag and wanted the privilege of taking his comrade away, which Captain Blackburn gave him.

The next morning when we got to camp, we found the officers all around Jim, trying to buy his horse. It was a large bay stallion and the finest horse in the regiment, and Jim rode that horse through the war, and he has the saddle and bridle today to show his friends.

Well, in this attack was the first gun powder that I smelled, and the first man that I saw killed; so the very next day I wrote home that I had seen a fight. Not one of our men got hurt, so it could hardly be rated as a skirmish, but before the war was over, you may depend, I found out what a real battle meant.

Well, Jim had a horse again and everyone was praising him up, and this was the way he got it. After he left us, he never stopped running till he was a good mile from the bridge, then got down to a walk, and after going seven or eight miles, he came to a large plantation house where there were nine or ten horses tied to the fence. Jim crawled up close and soon saw that they were rebel's horses, and the rebs were still inside except one who was sitting on the porch keeping guard; or as Jim said, "talking to a mighty good-looking girl." Jim slipped along the fence, at the same time watching the porch, and when the two there got quite interested in each other, Jim slipped up, cut the hitching: strap, and was in the saddle and off like a shot. He got the best horse they had, and also got the horse from the same party that stole his horse. We found that out by a prisoner that was taken shortly after.

In about two weeks after this I was on picket at the long bridge again, when Jim came riding upon his fine horse. "Hello, Bill I have a pass to go over the bridge again." Well, Jim was honest this time. The doctor got a pass for him to go out for food for the sick soldiers, and there was no one in the regiment that could beat him for that. "Goodbye, Jim, don't let the rebs get that horse from you while you are sparking"

"Look out for yourself." Most every one of the boys had something to say to him as he crossed the bridge. He went straight up to St. Charles, rode up to the same house where he lost his horse. The same young lady was sitting where he last saw her, and he walked up to her, made a very polite bow and said, "How do you do, sis?"

And she replied, "I thought I told you never to come here again."

Jim looked at her and said: "Now look here; listen to me for one moment. In the first place I love you, and want you to be my wife. I have thought of you, and dreamed of you, and the fact is you are here between two contending armies; you are liable to be burned out, then you would have no place to go to. Now, way up north in Illinois I have a nice little home, and one of the best mothers living there all alone, out of hearing of the war; all is peace there, and I want to send you to my mother to be a daughter to her; I know she will love you for her son's sake, if nothing else."

What girl could resist such pleading from such a handsome young fellow as our Jim? She looked up at him and seeing he was in dead earnest said: "When would you want me to go?"

"Right away; there is a lady from our town who is going back tomorrow, and you can go right home with her."

"I will go in and see what mother says." She slipped in the house, while Jim stood twisting his hat in his hands as if he was going to make a rope of it. Presently the girl came to the door and told him to come in. which he did, and found the old lady sitting in a rocking chair. As Jim went in the old lady looked up and told him to be seated. She asked him a great many questions about his home and mother, to which Jim answered satisfactorily. The old lady stepped out so Jim and the girl could talk over their affairs alone.

Said she: "Young man, you are a stranger to me and an enemy to our cause; I do not even know your name, but I will marry you on two conditions—one is that you will let my mother go with me, and the other is that I am not to be your wife in the true sense of the word till this war is over, and then I want it understood that if I see anything in your character that is obnoxious to me, you are to bring me home here, and forever leave me alone," to which our Jim gave cheerful consent. They were married by a minister who lived close by, and Jim sent his wife and mother-in-law, up to Illinois, and just let me whisper in your ear, dear reader, they are there yet, (as at time of first publication), and you may depend there is not a nicer family for miles around.

# CHAPTER 4

# Selected for Dispatch Rider

One fine morning my captain told me to report to Colonel Brackett. I walked up to regimental headquarters. The colonel was writing when I stepped into the tent; he looked up and said, "Be seated for a moment." He soon got through with his writing, folded it up, put it in a large envelope and handed it to me, saying, "Sergeant, have you a good horse?" Now, my reader, excuse me if I was proud of my horse for there was not one in the regiment that could outrun or outjump mine. "Well," said the colonel, "You may need just such a horse before you get back to camp. I want you to take this dispatch to General Curtis, some thirty miles from here, and wait his orders." Anything of this kind just suited me, for I was fond of adventure. I went to headquarters and handed my dispatch to General Curtis; as he tore open the envelope he told me to stop a moment to see what it said. After he had read the contents, he looked me over from head to foot and finally asked, "What regiment do you belong to?"

"I belong to the Ninth Ill. Cavalry, Co. I."

"What is your name?"

"William N. Tyler."

"Well, I think you are the very man I want. I have a dispatch to send to Colonel Wyman, who is acting brigadier-general at Little Rock, Ark., one hundred and fifty miles south. Now the road is infested with rebels; are you willing to undertake it?"

"Yes, sir," said I.

"Well," said the colonel, "report to me in the morning and I will give you instructions and dispatches." General Curtis was a fatherly old man, but very strict. He was all of six feet high, gray eyes and hair. He was good to his men and did all he could to keep them in good health and well clothed, but would punish severely if any were caught foraging on their own hook. He gave me orders to report to a cavalry regiment and they would find me quarters for the night.

Early the next morning I was on hand but had to wait until almost noon before the general was ready for me. He handed me three large envelopes and said, "Now, Sergeant, I want you to take these dispatches to Colonel Wyman at Little Rock, and wait his orders. If you get in close quarters with the rebels and are in danger of being captured, be sure to destroy the dispatches. Whatever you do, don't let the rebs get them. My orderly will go across the river with you, and the captain out on picket post will instruct you when to start and what road to take." While the general was giving me my orders all the officers had their eyes bent on me, so you may be sure I was glad when the general gave the final order.

The orderly, and myself mounted our horses and rode down to the river. There was a pontoon bridge out for about two hundred yards, and the balance of the river was crossed by a ferry boat—what they called a rope ferry. It was run by means of a rope fastened from one shore to the other. The men on the boat would draw it by the rope from one side to the other. Just two days before I got there they were crossing with some artillery and horses, and as they were in the centre of the river the horses got frightened and became uncontrollable, capsizing the boat and drowning nine men and a number of horses. We got safely across and commenced to climb the mountain on the other side. Finally we reached the top and oh! what a sight met our eyes; we could see for miles around to the north, but to the south it was all hills and mountains.

My road lay directly south, so it proved a pretty rough one. When we got to the top of the mountain and looked down on

White River, I could not see how it was possible for our horses to haul the artillery up the mountain. It looked to me that a horse had all he could do to climb it without pulling anything. The picket post was on the summit of the mountain. The orderly that came with me took the captain to one side and had quite a long talk in an undertone and finally came back to me, reached out his hand and bade me goodbye and told me not to let the rebs get me. Then he went back again. The captain of the guard came up and told me to dismount. After giving my horse to a man, I went to where the guards were sitting around the fire. Some were cooking and some were telling stories. One tall fellow was telling about being kept in irons for four days. He looked up and saw me standing back a little and told me to come to the fire. "Stranger, the wind blows mighty cold up here on the mountain." I walked up and sat down, drank some coffee and ate hard tack and bacon, so had as good a dinner as if I had been in my own camp.

"So they have had you in irons four days?"

"Yes, you see the old general is mighty strict about our foraging, but the other day we got out of corn and it is very scarce around here, so we got orders for a few to go out at a time and scour the country for corn.

"Our sergeant took ten of us and we started out; rode two days and was just on the point of coming in with our corn when we met an old darkey who told us to follow an old blind road and we would find a farm house down there where there was plenty of corn. We went and found it just as he said, but only having one wagon it did not take long for us to fill it; then we looked around for something good to eat. I got one ham and a pig, which I put in a gunny sack and threw across my horse and started for camp. Well, my pig kept kicking and I cut a hole in the sack so he could breathe; then he put his nose through the hole so he could take a view of the surrounding country; after that he was quiet.

"We got into Batesville all right and just as we were passing General Curtis' headquarters my captain looked up and saw us coming. 'Hello, boys! where did you get your corn?' Of course that brought us to a halt. The captain looked around and saw me with my sack. 'John, what have you got in your sack?' 'Corn, sir,' said I, and just then that infernal pig stuck his nose through the hole and squealed; now, you bet that fixed me."

Just then the captain of the guard came up, told me to go with him and took me out to one side. "Now," said he, "I want to give you your directions." So he gave me very plain directions about the route, so I felt very confident that I would not have any trouble. "Now, you had better lie down and get all the rest you can. I will see that you are wakened up in proper time, and see that you are provided with rations, for you know it won't do for you to stop at houses for food."

I lay down, rolled up in my blanket with my feet to the fire and was soon sound asleep, and did not wake up till the captain of the guard gave me a good shake. "It is twelve o'clock, get up and have a cup of coffee." I got up at once and rolled up my blanket and was soon ready to start. The same darkey that took care of my horse was sent along to guide me. The boys that were awake all had something to say and the captain's last words were, "Take care of yourself, my boy."

We started. "Now," said the darkey, "no use your trying to ride in dis darkness, for de limbs of de trees brush you off from dat horse, sure." So I followed close to the darkey. It was just a narrow bridle path with blackberry bushes interlaced across it and branches of trees hung down so that I had some difficulty in getting my horse along.

Said I: "This path has not been travelled for years."

"Hush, you must keep as still as you can, for we are not a great way from dem rebel guards." That was the first I knew of getting around rebel guards, so you may be sure after that I went along as still as possible. On we went over fallen limbs, hour after hour, till it was broad daylight. My clothes were covered with burs from head to foot, so I got the darkey to scrape them off with a knife and came out on the main road. "Now, mister, I is gone wid you as far as I can go; so you must follow dis main road straight south. Goodbye, sir, hope you will get through all right."

I led my horse out in the middle of the road, examined my carbine and revolver and found them all loaded and in good order. I mounted and turned south and jogged along slowly so as to keep my horse fresh," so if I had to I could make a good run. Over hills and lofty mountains I went all the forenoon and not a Johnnie did I see. I went back from the road about half a mile right in the heavy timber at noon, and made a cup of coffee and fed my horse with the only feed of corn I had with me. Went back on the road and on we went until dark. I had travelled all day and not a living thing had I seen except now and then a squirrel or rabbit. I was now looking for a place to camp.

Finally I came to an old blind road that led off in the timber; after following this road for about two miles, I was just thinking about going in the brush and camping for the night, when all at once I saw a light ahead. The first thought was that there was a rebel camp. I took my horse out in the thick brush and tied him to a small tree, and crawled on all fours till I got up close to the light, and found it to be a small cabin. The clay, from between the logs had fallen out and there was a bright fire burning in the fireplace, and it was the light of the fire shining through the cracks. I looked through and saw a large fleshy negro woman sitting in front of the fire smoking a corn-cob pipe and humming over some camp melody. I stepped up to the open door and said, "Good evening, aunty." I thought for a fact she would jump out of her skin.

"For de Lord sake, honey, how you scare me; who is you?"

"Aunty, are there any white folks close around here?"

"No, honey, no one lives close; no one lives here except me and my old man and he's gone out to catch a possum."

"Then there are no soldiers that come here?"

"No honey, der been no soldier here since de war begun."

"Well, aunty," said I, "can I stay here tonight?"

"Course you can."

"Have you got any corn for my horse?"

"Course we have; we'uns got a cow and we always keep fodder and corn both."

I went back, got my horse and put him in an old shanty back of the house and gave him a good feed of corn and fodder. When I went in after taking care of my horse old aunty was bustling around getting supper. Just then the old man stepped in. He had an old flint-lock gun in one hand and in the other he had a possum, sure enough. The negro was all of six feet in height and was just the opposite of aunty. He looked as if the wind would blow him away. His gun was as long as himself and looked as if it had been made in the year of one, it was so battered up. The stock had been broken many times and tied up with strings, and the old darkey looked about the same as his gun. No shoes on his feet, and oh! such feet it hasn't been my lot to see for many a day. His ankle was right in the middle of his foot. When he saw me I do not think I ever saw anyone more astonished than he was then. His eyes looked like two peeled onions, he commenced to open his mouth and the more he looked the wider it opened. "Well, uncle," said I, "What do you think of me?"

"Well," said he, shutting his mouth, "I don't know."

I thought we were in the same boat as far as that was concerned. Old aunty walked up to him, snatched the possum out of his hand, gave him a smart box on the ear and said: "Ain't you got no manners? standin' der wid yer mouf open as wide as a barn door! You don't know nuffin; you make me awful 'shamed. Now, you go and sit down dere and don't open dat big mouf of yours till supper. Does ye heah?" I think he heard, for let me tell you, when she opened her mouth you would think there was a cyclone coming.

It did not take aunty long to take the skin off that possum and clean it. She soon had it in the skillet with sweet potatoes.

Old aunty passed close to me and saw my saber. "Oh," said she, "What's dat?" I told her that the right name for it was saber, but most of the boys called it a cheese knife. "For de Lawd sake, is dat what you cut cheese wid?" I explained its use to her, after which she asked me if I was a Yankee soldier. I answered in the affirmative. "Now, is dat so? My old marster told me that you'ns had horns."

Now, it may be that the reader will think this overdrawn, but let me say that most any of my comrades will corroborate my statement when I say that not only did the negroes think that the Yankees had horns, but there were a great many white folks who would tell us the same thing; I remember on one of our foraging trips we came up to a very nice farmhouse, and an old lady came out and said, "Are you'ns Yankees? why, I thought they had horns."

After old aunty got her curiosity satisfied she stepped to the door and got two large ears of corn and walked up to the fireplace and threw them into the fire.

"What are you doing that for?" I asked.

"I is goin' to make coffee out of dat corn. Don't you like coffee?"

"Yes, but I have better coffee than that."

"Good Lord! has you got store coffee?"

"Yes." So I went out to my saddle-bags and brought in a large drawing of coffee. The negroes were highly delighted to get some coffee, and so was I to get as good a supper as I got that night. Reader, if you ever want a good meal go south and let some old black aunty cook you some sweet potatoes and possum together.

The next morning, after I had my breakfast, I went and got all the coffee I had except one drawing, and gave it to the old woman. I asked her how they came to be living away out there alone.

"Well, I tell you: my old man is the rail-splitter, and my old master sent us to split rails, and dat is all we does."

# CHAPTER 5

# A Very Close Call

I thanked the old lady for her kindness and rode back to the road again, went over hills, forded creeks, passed farmhouses, but not a rebel did I see. I began to think there were no rebels in that part of the country, consequently got careless, and through my carelessness came within one of losing my life.

It was almost twelve o'clock. Right ahead of me a little way in the valley that I was descending to was a large frame house that stood close to the road, and beyond this house about fifty yards was a creek that went across the road, but no bridge over it. Now, I thought this would be a good place to eat dinner, so I rode down to the creek, watered my horse and as there was a large shade tree standing in front of the house I went back, dismounted, took the saddle off, wiped off my horse and put the saddle back on. I had brought corn from where I stayed all night. I took off the bridle and put the feed bag on my horse's nose and was about to eat my own dinner when, glancing around, I saw a negro standing by the little gate. Said he: "Master, are you a Union soldier?"

"Yes, sir."

"I thought so; well, sir, you is in a mighty bad fix. My master is in the house and he is captain, and he has fifteen soldiers with him, and way up on de top of dat hill is a whole regiment of confederates, and they expect some more every minute on the same road dat you came on. But see here now: you go straight through dat creek and you will find a bridle path that turns to the left. You go on that path till you come to the fence; go over the fence and down over the hill till you get down in a cornfield, den you can come by this same road again."

While the negro was telling me which way to go, you may depend I was not idle; I pulled the feed-bag off of that horse's nose and had the bridle on sooner than you could say "Jack Robinson." Now this rebel captain was watching every move I made. He turned to his men and said, "Now watch me and see how slick I will capture a Yankee."

Reader, I will soon tell you how I found out what the rebel captain said. Just as I had got the bridle on, the captain stepped out with a double-barrelled shot-gun, (and I think the gun must have been loaded half full, the way it sounded) and said: "Surrender! you Yankee son-of-a-gun," Do not think that I am trying to make myself out brave, but let me tell you it was fight or die. My horse stood straight between the captain and me, and to snatch my carbine from the saddle was the work of a second, and I brought it to my shoulder. Just as my horse swung out of the way both guns went off together. The bullet from my gun struck the stock of his and glanced off into his shoulder and knocked him down. I was on my horse in a flash and through the creek we went. The negro told me afterwards that the water flew thirty feet high. I found the path all right, but had to lie down close to my horse to prevent the branches from sweeping me off.

Away we went. I soon came to a fence and threw the rails down and started up the hill. I was obliged to lead my horse to the top, the hill being so steep. Just as I got to the top the Johnnies were at the bottom, and commenced firing up. When I got to the bottom of the other side of the hill, they were at the top and commenced firing down. Close to the bottom was a creek with very steep banks. My horse did not want to go through and I coaxed and whipped all to no effect. I was about to leave my horse, when "*zip*" came a bullet and struck him on the shoulder. He made a sprint forward, almost jerking the bridle strap out of my hand. Through the stream he plunged and came within one of getting away from me. The corn was just up to my shoulders, and when I got started I do not believe I ever rode so fast in my life. The corn whipped my feet as if someone was striking me with a cane.

In the meantime the Johnnies had got to the bottom of the hill and were blazing away at me with all their might. One bullet went through the rim of my hat and another through my coat sleeve. Finally, I came to a fence again. Right ahead of me was a low place in it and over we went. When my horse struck the ground I was all of a foot above him, and came down on the crupper. I made a grab for the saddle and saved myself from a fall, and I came near losing my horse again.

I was out in the road once more ahead of all the rebels, and rode on for half a mile, stopped, dismounted and tightened up the girth. The blood was oozing out of the wound in my horse's hip. I looked back up the hill and saw the rebels coming again. I knew they had no horse that could catch me if the wound did not affect him. I kept a good mile ahead of them, but every time they got to the top of a hill they would blaze away at me.

About five o'clock, my horse commenced to get lame and I began to think I was gone up. I looked up on the hill ahead of me, and saw soldiers walking back and forth across the road. I reached into my pocket for the dispatches to destroy them when two men rose up from behind the fence and brought their gun to bear on me and said, "Don't destroy those papers." I was caught. I saw that they both had blue coats on, but there were lots of rebels who wore blue clothes.

I asked, "What regiment do you belong to?"

"We belong to the Thirteenth Illinois Infantry," they said. I never was so glad to see blue coats in my life. The rebels came to the top of the hill behind me and stopped. They could see that I had got to our guards. They fired one volley and retreated. In the meantime, our boys had formed a line across the road, but did not waste powder by returning the fire. I rode up to the captain of the guard, and told him I had dispatches for Colonel Wyman. He told me to dismount, and get a cup of coffee, and he would see whether the wound my horse received was serious or not.

I rubbed him down and gave the poor fellow some food. The boys in blue got around me, asking all sorts of questions about my trip, and I gave them my experience from Jacksonport. They all listened very much interested.

Finally, one of the men who was standing close to me said, "I'll be darned if there isn't a bullet hole through your hat rim." As the guard was five miles from the main camp, and my horse was played out, I stayed all night, and the next morning rode into camp, up to Colonel Wyman's headquarters and delivered my dispatches. When I first started in the morning, my horse walked lame, but after we had gone a mile or two he did not seem to mind it. The colonel read over the dispatch and looked at me from head to foot. "Well, did you see any of the Johnnies on your trip from Batesville down?"

"Yes, sir."

"Well" said he, "the dispatches you brought order me with a brigade back to Batesville. We start back in the morning and you go to our veterinary surgeon and let him see to your horse and you rest today, and tomorrow you may go with us back to Batesville, and when you get to where the rebel captain fired on you, let me know."

As I was wandering around the tent I found my brother-in-law, Lewis Stafford, and had a good visit with him. The surgeon told me that my horse would soon be all right.

The next morning, bright and early, everyone was in motion. There were about five thousand troops, cavalry, artillery and infantry. We soon got on the road where the Johnnies gave me such a close rub. All at once there was firing in front. It did not amount to much, just a small skirmish; two poor fellows were brought back wounded. The first night we camped within five miles of where the rebel captain fired on me. The next day about 10 o'clock we came up on a high hill and at the bottom was the plantation house. I recognized it at once as being the one where the rebel captain tried to show his men how slick he could capture a Yankee. I rode up to Colonel Wyman and pointed it out to him. "All right," said he, "you stay with me and we will make a neighbourly call on him." We rode up under the same tree where I was going to feed my horse, and dismounted; walked up on the porch and the same negro stood there.

"My Lord! Is dat you? Dem soldiers dun told me dat day hang vou on a tree."

"Is your master in?"

"Yes, sir, you broke his shoulder all to pieces." He opened the door and led us in; the captain lay on a couch, but had not had his wound dressed and it had become very painful. One of the men said:

"You are wounded."

"Yes," (with an oath) "there was a Yankee scout who came along the other day, and he was just one second too quick for me."

"Here is the man now," said our colonel.

The rebel captain looked at me and reached out his well arm and said, "Shake, stranger, you are a good soldier."

The colonel sent and had our surgeon dress his wound properly and said, "Now, you are fixed all right. You can stay here and no one will molest you, or you can go with us and have proper treatment."

"Well," said the rebel captain, "let me take my nigger along and I will go where I can get proper treatment."

They put him in an ambulance and took him along. The nigger told me all the particulars as we went along the road. He said his master's gun went off up in the air, that he hadn't got it pointed at me at all.

We got to Batesville all right. I went up to General Curtis' headquarters and reported. He gave me a dispatch to take to Colonel Brackett, Ninth Illinois Cavalry, my own regiment, back to Jacksonport. I was glad to go back to my own regiment again. It was like getting home. I had no mishap but got there all right, went to headquarters and delivered my dispatch. "You have got back," said the colonel. "Take a rest today, for tomorrow I will send you out on a foraging expedition."

The men were all glad to see me, and they all wanted to go

out foraging with me the next day. They wanted to know all about my trip. I received two letters from home, and my folks were all well, so I felt all right.

Just as I had finished reading my letters Colonel Brackett sent word for me to come to headquarters. I went. He told me to be seated.

"I have a letter from General Curtis here that you brought in the dispatches, that praises you very highly. He said you were every inch a soldier. I have changed my mind in regard to sending you out on a foraging expedition. We have lost two very fine artillery horses, and I heard that they were some forty miles north of here. You take one man and start in the morning. Come to headquarters, and in the meantime I will ascertain which way you are to go."

# CHAPTER 6

# The Government Horses

I ran back to my tent, and just then Jim Carlysle came along.

"Jim, you are the very man I am looking for. I want you to be ready to go with me in the morning."

I explained what was wanted, and he expressed a desire to go. I went up to headquarters, and the colonel gave me a piece of paper with the man's name on that had the horses.

"Now, look sharp," said the colonel, "it may be a trap to catch you."

After getting instructions about the road, we started and crossed the long bridge five miles north of camp, and kept on until noon. Finally we came to a double log cabin. We rode up to it, dismounted, stepped to the door and knocked. For the benefit of the readers who never travelled south, I want to explain. All the houses if ever so small, have a porch in front. The double log houses are built separately, about ten or twelve feet apart, the roof covering the whole building. The chimney is built on the outside of the house, generally one on each end. They are built of stone or brick, about ten feet from the ground. The balance of the way they are built of clay and sticks. A lady stepped to the door and told us to come in. I asked her if we could get some dinner.

"O, yes; of course you can."

The lady proved to be a Union woman. She was a widow. There were any number of Union widows all over the south.

They had husbands who were in the rebel army, but every time any of our forces were around they would claim to be Union women and call for protection, and do not forget it, our officers were always on hand for protection.

She gave us chairs and told us to be seated. She was a great talker, and asked us if we were married, and if we had children. Jim told her that he hadn't been married long. Then she wanted to know if his wife was pretty and any amount of similar questions. All the time she was getting dinner her tongue was running. She told us that she had a large farm, was out of debt, and if she could get some real good man she didn't know but that she might be induced to marry again. I asked her if she knew of a man up north twenty or thirty miles by the name of Smith, for that was the man who had our horses. She said she had heard of the name. We then settled for our dinners, mounted our horses and rode on.

We had not gone over a mile before we came to a swamp. It was about two miles through. It had a corduroy bridge, that is, logs about two feet in diameter, and twelve feet long, laid side by side. The water was about eighteen inches deep. Some of the logs were floating. When our horses stepped on them they would sink. We went on until we got about halfway across, and came to a place where three of the logs had floated out. If by accident our horses should get in the swamp, it would be almost impossible to get them out. You could take a ten-foot rail and push it the entire length in the mud. We got down from our horses and after about two hours' work, got the logs back to their places.

Away off in the timber we heard the distant sound of thunder. The air was stifling. The trees on each side of the bridge interlaced overhead. It was almost dark, so we had to ride very slowly. The road was getting worse and worse, and clouds had covered the whole heavens. About three o'clock it began to get dangerous to ride, so we dismounted and led our horses. There came a flash of lightning, and we could see that we were almost over the swamp. Great drops of rain began to fall.

"There is a house," said Jim. Sure enough we were over the swamp and close to a large house.

We had just got in a large log barn when the storm broke in all its fury. You could hardly see twenty feet, the trees falling in every direction. For two whole hours the storm raged. In all my experience I do not think I ever saw so much water fall in so short a time. It began to get lighter and lighter; we could see small patches of blue sky, and finally it ceased raining. When the sun came out again it was pretty well down in the west.

"Well, Jim, you wait here and I will go in and see if we can stay here tonight." I walked up to the house and was just turning the corner when two large hounds made a jump at me. To draw my saber was the work of a second. We always carry our pistols in our saddles, and consequently I did not have mine with me. The dogs kept just out of reach until one made a jump at me and almost got me by the legs. I brought my saber down across his back and almost cut him in two. *Crack!* went a pistol. I looked around and there stood Jim with a smoking revolver in his hand, and the other dog lay quivering on the ground.

"By thunder! Bill," said Jim, "Those dogs would have got away with you."

"I was almost tired out; yes, and the old man was looking out of the window all the time, and never made one effort to call them off."

"Well, let us both go in."

We never waited to rap, but opened the door and walked in. An elderly man, probably fifty, sat in a chair, and a young lady sat on the opposite side of the fireplace sewing.

"How do you do, strangers."

"Why did you not call off your dogs?"

"Well, sir, those dogs were mine, and they were kept on purpose to keep such fellows as you off."

"Well, old man, they failed that time, and let me tell you that just such fellows as we want to stay here all night, and would like to have the young lady get us some supper, Jim, you go see to the horses and get my carbine and revolver."

The girl looked up to her father to see what he had to say. The old man looked at us and said:

"Do you call yourselves gentlemen and force yourselves upon us?"

"Now, that has nothing to do with the case. Do you call yourself a gentleman and stand and see your dogs tear a man to pieces? There is only one thing about this matter: I want to know, miss, if you will get us some supper."

"Yes, sir," said the girl, "If pa says so."

"Well," said the old man, "You might as well get them something to eat, for if you don't they might burn the house down."

Just then Jim came in. It was now getting dusk.

"Jim, you stay here to watch the old man and I will go out and see how things look around here. Don't let him go out of the room, and keep an eye on the girl, too."

I went all around the place, and back close to the timber were two negro shanties. I stepped up to one and knocked.

"Come in, sir."

I walked in. There were eight or nine negroes sitting around, from a little baby to an old, white-haired man. The old man raised up and said:

"How do you do, sir; will you sit down on this bench?"

"No, thank you; I have no time to sit down. I would like to know if there are any Confederate soldiers camped around here."

"No, sir; dar am no soldiers camped around dis place, and habn't been for two weeks, and da was Union soldiers dat was here two weeks ago."

"I suppose your master is a Union man, isn't he?"

"No, sir; I is sorry to say that he is the hardest kind of a rebel. His two boys are in de rebel army; and, sir, as soon as he found out that you were here, he made me go let the dogs loose. Dem dogs cost my master five hundred dollars. Dey was de best bloodhounds in dis part of the country."

"Well, sir, I'm very much obliged for your information," and turned to go.

44

"Hold on, mister. For de Lord's sake, don't tell master dat I tole you anything!"

I went back to the house and Jim was standing by the door, watching every move that was made. The girl had supper ready.

Keep your carbine in your lap while you eat," said I, and we sat up to the table and ate a good, hearty supper.

"Now, old man, we do not wish to abuse you or your family, but are going to stay here tonight, and if we see any treachery on your part your life won't be worth a cent. Now, Jim, you go to bed and I will wake you up promptly at twelve o'clock."

There being a bedroom close at hand Jim went in and was soon snoring like a bugle call. The girl could not restrain a smile at his snoring. The old man sat smoking his pipe, casting glances over to where I sat. Finally he broke out and said:

"Now, look here, stranger, do you think you are going to sit there and bulldoze me all night and make me sit here?"

"No, sir, you can go to bed just as soon as you please, but I want to see where you sleep."

"You can't see where I or my daughter sleeps, and I want you to distinctly understand it!"

"All right, old man, you will stay just where you are, then."

He jumped, to his feet and said, "I will not do it for any Yankee living."

I cocked my gun and brought it to bear on the old man and said:

"Make a move and you are a dead man. And, miss, you sit there, too."

The old fellow turned as white as a sheet and dropped back into the chair as if he had been shot.

"Now, sir, the best thing you both can do is to keep quiet and not a hair of your head shall be harmed."

Hour after hour passed until the clock struck one. The old man and his daughters were both nodding in their chairs. I waked Jim and told him to watch so the old fellow would not be playing any games on us. I went to bed and to sleep, and did not awake till sunrise. There was an old negro woman bustling around getting breakfast. We told the man and his daughter they could go anywhere in the house, but they must not go out until we left. The old man jumped to his feet and turned on me like a wildcat and said:

"You will pay dearly for last night's work."

"All right; you need not think that we are going to give you a chance to inform your Confederate friends. You know this is all fair in war times. Jim, go see to the horses while I watch."

He soon returned and said that the horses were all right. We then sat down to the breakfast table without waiting for an invitation. Jim asked the old man if he wouldn't sit up and have some breakfast with us. The man snorted out with an oath,

"I would die before I would eat with a Yank."

Old aunty's eyes rolled around like saucers, and she said, "May de good Lord hab mercy on us all."

The girl sat and watched every move, but had nothing to say. We finished our breakfast and started for the door, when Jim turned around and made a very polite bow and said:

"We are much obliged for your kindness, and if you ever come our way, be sure and call on us." We then mounted and went on; the road was full of branches of trees and fence rails, so we had some trouble getting our horses along. As we got out into the road, we looked back over the swamp; it was a perfect sea of water. The logs had floated out and left great gaps in the road so it was impossible to go back the same way we came. We finally came out to a more thickly settled portion of the country, and found the roads a great deal better and the people seemed to be more communicative. They told us the man, Smith, lived only a short distance ahead of us, so we got to his house about noon and found the horses all right. The house stood off from the road about a half a mile. We rode up in front of the house. There were eight or ten negro buildings all around the main building. The gentleman came out to meet us in the door yard. "Is your name Smith?"

"Yes, sir."

"Have you got a couple of government horses here?"

"Yes, sir."

"Well, we have come after them and you are to come to Jacksonport and our quartermaster will pay you for your trouble."

We found Mr. Smith to be a true gentleman, and a true Union man. He said he did not want any pay, that he wanted to do something for Uncle Sam. He called on an old darkey to come for the horses, and told him to feed the horses and take good care of them.

"Now, you men stay here all night and by morning the water will be down in the swamps so you will be able to get back all right. He told us of another way to go back that would take us around the big swamp. We concluded to stay, for it did seem to be quite a rest to get among Union people.

Now, my dear reader, let me tell you that when we did come across Union people in the south they were genuine. We were in a Union neighbourhood; the last rebel we passed was the man we stayed all night with. Mr. Smith told us that if we hadn't watched the man he would have played some underhanded trick on us. The next morning we started back to Jacksonport and travelled until noon, each leading a horse. We stopped at a farmhouse and got our dinner, then travelled on till night. We could see that there was another storm coming up fast, but luckily a plantation house came in view and we just reached it as the rain began to fall. The owner of the house came out and told us to come in, which we did, leaving our horses in the care of a darkey.

Although the man was a rebel from the top of his head to the sole of his foot, he told us that we were perfectly welcome to his house and that we were just as safe there as if we had been in our own camp. I must say that he used us well; we hadn't been there over half an hour before supper was announced. The man introduced us to his family. There were three grown up daughters and the old lady. They had only one son, and he was in the army. As they told us this, the tears started from the mother's eyes and the girls looked as if they were ready to cry, too. We ate our supper in silence, then went to the sitting room and talked until bedtime. The next morning we offered to pay him, but he would take nothing. We then resumed our journey and ended it just at twelve o'clock. We got to camp, rode up to headquarters and reported to Colonel Brackett.

"Well, sergeant, we were about to send a company out to look for you, as we began to think that the rebs had got you."

# CHAPTER 7

# Gunboats, Bushwackers and Johnnies

The 21st of June, just the day before we got back to camp with the horses, one of our scouts reported a rebel gunboat to come up the river, so Colonel Brackett gave me orders to take ten men and go five miles below Jacksonport and watch for the boat. In the meantime the camp moved to the piece of land that divides the Black from the White River. We went below Jacksonport to the place stated and settled near a bend in the river where we had a good view of the river four or five miles. We had not been there long before we saw the black smoke rolling up away down the river. We waited until she rounded the bend, then fired off our carbines as we had orders and started back to camp.

The inhabitants of Jacksonport had professed to be Union people, but as soon as they heard that a rebel gunboat was coming up they altered their tune and called us all the mean names they could think of. Our officers had even put guards over their wells so as to keep the soldiers away. One woman in particular had given our officers a great deal of trouble. She was a good Union woman at that, and a widow. She wanted a guard to keep the soldiers off her premises, and our officers were just fools enough to do it.

Well, we were the last soldiers to go through the town, and, let me tell you, the gunboat was coming faster than we had any idea of. Just before we reached the town she sent a shell over our heads. We soon got in shelter of the town, and the citizens commenced to yell at us. Some said one thing and some another. Finally we came up in front of where the widow lived. She was out on the porch dressed in all her finery. As we were passing she called out:

"Is that what you Yankees call skedaddling?" One of our men turned in his saddle and said something that made her skip in the house in a hurry.

We rode on until we got to the ferry, which was nothing but an old scow of a boat. We were soon on the boat, and in the meantime the gunboat had swung around and commenced throwing shells at us. The first shell went over us; the next struck the water a hundred yards from us, and the third struck close and threw the water all over us. Our horses became unmanageable. One jumped overboard and the rest came near upsetting the boat. The one that jumped overboard swam to shore all right. We landed our horses and one man went back in a small boat and got it and cut the rope.

We had two large twelve-pound brass guns, and never fired a shot at the boat. I never did understand why they did not. But I know this much about it, we were ordered to mount and get out of there. We went back about eight or ten miles and met troops coming to reinforce us. The next morning we went back to Jacksonport, but found the gunboat gone.

There was a large quantity of sugar stored at this place, and the Johnnies rolled out the hogsheads and spilt the sugar in the middle of the road. Our horses waded knee deep in sugar for two hundred yards. The farmers came in droves and shovelled the sugar into their wagons like sand.

That night it rained. The ditches on both sides of the road were full of molasses. The citizens had a little more manners when we came back; there were no more guards put over wells, and not so much punishing going on if one of our men was caught foraging on his own hook.

In a few days after this there were two companies sent out foraging, and sometime in the afternoon we heard firing in the direction the foragers had gone. "Boots and saddles" were sounded and the balance of the Ninth was on their way to re-inforce. We soon came up with the teamsters who were driving for "dear life." We passed them and came up to where our men had formed a line. The rebels had also formed a line about three hundred yards in advance, and were crowding our men back, but as soon as we reinforced our men it turned the tide of the skirmish. We drove them back. I do not think it lasted over half an hour and after we got through we had forty men wounded and three killed outright. This occurred June 12th, 1862, and was the first time I had been in a skirmish. The rebels were mostly armed with double-barrelled shot-guns. Their loss was eleven killed and thirty wounded. We then went back to camp.

Skirmishing now became almost an everyday occurrence. Two companies were started on a foraging expedition down White River. After they got ten or twelve miles below Jacksonport two companies of rebels came up on the other side. As soon as they came in sight of one another they opened fire. The river at this point was five hundred yards across. Finally the rebels ceased firing, and one tall rebel stepped out from behind a tree and hollered over to our men and said:

" I will dare any single Yank to step out and have a fair, open stand up and fight with me, and we are to keep on firing until one goes down."

Out jumped our Jim. "All right, Johnnie, are you ready?" Now, both sides eased firing and looked on with interest. Jim was a splendid shot, and as cool as if shooting at a target. Both guns went off at once. The Johnnie called over, "Are you hit, Yank"

"Not by a darned sight. Are you?"

"I'm all right, Yank."

Jim took particular pains in loading. Both brought their guns to the ground together, reached and got a cartridge together, and pulled their ramrods together. The Johnnie pulled his out with a jerk and it flew ten feet away. By the time he had regained it and straightened up, Jim's gun was loaded. He brought it to his shoulder, took steady aim and fired. The rebel brought his hand to his breast with a slap and down he went. Just at this moment the rebels got a large reinforcement with artillery, and we were forced to fall back. A few days after, a rebel deserter came to our camp and told us that the rebel who fought Jim was in a fair way to get well, and that the bullet had struck in the centre of a large package of letters that he had in his breast pocket and only made a slight flesh wound.

We they returned to camp. It was getting late in the summer, and the country was infested with small bands of guerrillas. A great many of them were fighting on their own hook, that is, they were nothing but robbers. They robbed the southern and Union people, and if they happened to run onto a small company of Union soldier's whom they could overpower by numbers, and take them prisoners, they would march them out into the woods and shoot them. Such fellows never came out in an open fight, but were always sneaking around in the brush, and that is what gave them the name of bushwhackers. If by accident one of our men was caught alone by the bushwhackers we never heard of him again. They would take him out in the woods and shoot him, pull off his clothes, and leave his body to be devoured by turkey-buzzards, and that is why so many rebel soldiers were dressed in blue.

The women folks were even worse than the men; they poisoned the wells, and poisoned provisions and left them where our boys could easily find them, and at the same time rebel planters would call on our generals for protection. As sure as they found out that our army was coming that way, they would want a protection guard to keep the Yanks off their premises, and our officers would almost always grant their request.

One nice morning I had orders to report to headquarters. As I came up in front of headquarters tent. Colonel Brackett came out with a letter in his hand and said:

"Sergeant, you are ordered to take two men and go ten miles up the White River to a planter's house and to guard the property while some of General Curtis' men are passing. Allow no soldier on his premises."

I did not like that kind of a job, but orders had to be obeyed;

so I went down to camp and found Jim and a comrade by the name of Thorne, and started for the old Reb's plantation. We got there all right, rode up to the front of the house and dismounted. There were two men sitting on the porch, one a gray-headed man and the other a young man. They proved to be father and son. As I went in the gate two young ladies came out on the porch, followed by a coloured woman carrying chairs for them. When we first rode up, I noticed that when the young man saw we were Union soldiers he was very uneasy. I stepped upon the first step and raised my hat and asked who was the proprietor. The old gentleman said, "I am."

I handed him a letter and he opened it and examined it a long time, and finally called to one of the girls and said:

"Come here, Mary, and see if you can make this out."

"No, pa, I can't make it out at all."

"Then the old man turned to me and said, "It may be, stranger, that you can read this," at the same time handing me the letter.

"Well, sir, this is what it says: 'General Curtis sends his compliments to you and sends guards to protect your property while the Union army is passing.'"

"Oh, you are the guards?"

In a little while a young darkey appeared, and the man told -him to show the gentlemen where to put the horses. I told Jim to see that they were taken care of. As they disappeared around the house the old man invited me to take a chair which old aunty had provided for me. No sooner had I taken the chair than the old gentleman began telling me how mean our men had served him; stole his chickens and pigs, and, said he,

"I am a Union man, and my son here is also, and of course we want protection."

Just at this moment Thorne and Jim came around with the arms. Jim handed me my revolver and carbine. The house was the double log kind, with a kind of hall between the two houses, and a porch running the whole length of both parts, facing the road, and stood back from the road about twenty yards.

Away around a bend in the road to the right over a cornfield we could see the dust rolling up over the corn, as if a lot of horsemen were coming. Said I, "Mister, supposing they are confederates, what are we to do?"

"Oh, you're all right. I'll see that you are not hurt."

Then I knew that he was no Union man, or he would have no influence with the Rebs; for be it known that there was not a Union man in the south but what was spotted, and was as much hated as we hated the copperheads of the north. I could see that the young man was watching the cloud of dust with great interest. One of the girls jumped to her feet and went in and brought out a field-glass. The troops now began to come around the bend in the road.

"They are Confederates," said the girl.

"Our orders were to stay until our troops passed, so there was no alternative for us but to stay. There were about seven hundred Confederates, and all mounted. They rode up in front of the house, and the planter and his family all walked out to the fence. The rebel colonel dismounted, and we could see that they were talking earnestly about us, for they cast glances our way quite often. The rebel soldiers were yelling at us, wanting to know if we had any horses to trade. The rebel colonel made a motion for me to advance. I stepped out to the gate.

"To what regiment do you belong," the colonel asked.

"I belong to the Ninth Illinois Cavalry."

"Where are you stationed?" he asked.

"I'm stationed at Jacksonport."

"How many are there of you?"

"Do you take me for a fool?" said I.

"Oh no, I take you for a Yankee soldier. This gentleman told me that you were sent as a protection guard, and I want to tell you that you are perfectly safe, as far as we are concerned. Do you know when your men are to pass here?"

"I do not know anything about it." By this time quite a number of the soldiers had got over the fence and were talking to Jim and Thorne. It was getting late in the afternoon, and away off in the west could be heard distant thunder. The colonel ordered them to mount, and they rode on about half a mile and went into camp. I noticed that the young man went with them.

Every move that was made by the family we were guarding showed them to be rebels. The great, black clouds came rolling up from the west. The lightning was something fearful to behold, and the deep bass thunder shook the earth to its very foundation. The negroes were running in every direction. It could easily be seen that they were terribly frightened at the approaching storm. Great drops of rain began to fall.

"Just then the rebel colonel and two captains came riding up, threw themselves from the saddle and told the darkey to put their horses under shelter. As the darkey was leading the horses there came a flash of lightning, and a deafening crash of thunder followed so closely that it seemed more like the noise of a cannon. One of the horses rose up on his hind feet and struck the darkey with his front feet and sent him sprawling on the ground. At that all three started up to the rebel camp on a run and disappeared round a bend in the road. The old gentleman was standing out on the porch. He spoke to another darkey and told him to go and see if Sam was dead. Just then Sam rose to a sitting position and looked up and saw us gazing at him and hollered out,

"Oh, massa, I is dunderstruck!"

The rain now began to pour down and the wind was blowing fearfully. The darkey jumped to his feet and made for a place of shelter. We all went into the house, it was getting quite dark. They were obliged to light candles. In a few minutes a coloured woman came to the door and announced supper.

"Now," said the old gentleman, "I want you Confederates and you Federals to come and eat at the same table, and I want it understood that there is to be no quarrelling."

As we filed into the dining room we laid our arms in one corner of the room and sat down to the table. I sat next to a rebel captain, and the rebel colonel and the two girls sat opposite us. Every time that the captain who sat next to me had

55

anything to say it was a slur on the Yankees. The rebel colonel did not approve of his actions, for he frequently shook his head at him. Finally the captain said:

"I believe I could lick twenty Yanks alone. I know I could if they were all like these we have here."

I turned to the old gentleman and said:

"We came here to guard you and your family and not to be insulted."

"Well," said the old man, "I am very sorry this has occurred."

"Well," said Jim, "It was not two weeks ago that one of your men challenged one of our men to come out and have a square stand-up fight across White River. He probably thought he could get away with twenty Yankees too, but, Mr. Reb, I went out and had a fair fight with him and got away with him, too, so if you think you can get away with twenty Yanks such as are here, you can try me in the morning. If you get away with me, you will have two more to try your hand on."

The old gentleman jumped up and said,

"I want this thing stopped, and want it distinctly understood that there will be no fighting here."

We finished our supper in silence, and as we were rising to leave the table, I said,

"My opinion is, you will all get all the fighting you want before tomorrow night;" and I proved to be a good prophet that time.

# CHAPTER 8

# Cavalry Sergeant to Infantryman

We went back in the other room and talked over the prospects of the war without any hard feelings. The rebel captain had gone off with the girls. The colonel said, "I will put a guard around the house tonight. We do not want you men to go away until we move on."

I looked out and saw that the storm was over. The old gentleman told us we could go to bed any time, so it being ten o'clock, we took our arms and followed the old man upstairs. He took us into a room where there were two beds, put the candle on a stand, bade us goodnight and left us alone.

"Now," said Thorne, "I don't like the looks of things here. That rebel captain means mischief."

"Well," said Jim, "That old colonel is all right; he will keep that captain straight, you can bet on that."

Soon after we got in bed, I heard someone talking in the room below us. I slid out of bed slyly and pulled a piece of the carpet away and discovered a large knot hole in the floor. I made a sign for the boys to keep quiet while I looked through the hole. The rebel captain sat there with his arm around the girl's waist and she had her head on his shoulder. She was talking to him about us and this is what she said:

"That Yankee told the truth when he said he had a square fight with one of our men."

"Yes, the man he fought belonged to my company. He is in camp now and a better marksman cannot be found in the regiment. Now, my dear, can't we study up some plan to get away with these Yanks?"

"No, pa won't let us do anything, for you know he has fifty thousand dollars in gold buried down in one corner of the cellar, and if he did not have a protecting guard, the Yanks might go through the house and find it. I know it is hard and mean to have the dirty things here, but I suppose we will have to stand it."

"I will tell you how we can fix them in the morning. Treat everybody to some of that nice peach brandy of yours, and put a good dose of arsenic in the Yankees glasses, and you may be sure that will fix them."

"Do you really want me to do that?"

"Of course I do."

"What will pa say when General Curtis comes along and wants to know what has become of the guards he sent."

"You folks can say that they never came and he will just think they have deserted."

"But you know pa is so particular about his honesty, that he would spoil the whole thing."

"Your pa would not know what killed the Yanks, and we would take their horses and arms and your pa would be so frightened, that he would keep still."

"Well, what about your colonel?"

"Oh, the devil with him. I sometimes think he is half Yank by the way he acts and talks. Now, if you will kill these Yanks, you will be doing the Confederacy a great favour. It might not be three days before we get into a fight with them and they might kill your brother or me, so you see you can do as much as any soldier if you are brave and do what I want you to."

"Well, I will do it. For it may be as you say, and if my brother and you should be killed, I wouldn't want to live."

"Now you talk like my own brave little girl."

They had a good deal more to say that would not interest the reader. As long as we were in no immediate danger, I crawled back to bed and went to sleep. The next morning, when we woke up, I posted the boys about what I heard but there was no need of that, for away up toward the rebel camp we could hear the clash of fire arms—first one gun, then *bang!* came a shell right over the house. Everything was confusion in the house, women screaming, men cursing and negroes yelling. It was a perfect bedlam going on below.

It did not take long to go down and out on the stoop and look away up toward the rebel camp. The smoke of the battle was rising above the trees and the rebel colonel and the two captains were running up toward the conflict and soon disappeared around the bend in the road. The two girls came out on the porch, wringing their hands and crying. Just then there came another shell crashing through the air and struck in front of the house, ploughing a furrow in the ground and throwing dirt all over the porch. The girls skipped into the house and shut the door with a bang. The fire now became a steady roll. Here they come around the bend in the road. They are forming another line of battle, when *crack* comes another shell, striking through the top of the chimney, the brick and mortar flying in every direction.

Here comes the Johnnies again, the "Yanks" right after them. *Bang* at *bang, pop* at *pop!* See the Johnnies tumbling on every side! See the horses running pell-mell, without riders. Here they go right by the house, our brave boys in blue right after them. Round the cornfield they go, the fire growing fainter and fainter in the distance. Now the worst part is to come. They commence to bring in the wounded. The first to come was the rebel colonel, two of our men bearing him on a stretcher. His face was pinched and pale, with the blood oozing out of a wound in his breast. One of our surgeons came and gave me orders to bring in the wounded.

As we got on the road where the most desperate part of the battle took place, what a sight met our gaze. All kinds of arms scattered over the ground. Hats, caps and blankets, here a horse and there a horse, struggling in the agony of death, and men scattered all over the ground. Here a Yank and there a Reb, some dead, and others wounded. The rebels suffered the more, for they were taken wholly by surprise.

It was a regular cavalry fight. It was now about ten o'clock, and our infantry began to come up. It did not take long to get the wounded to where they could get care. Our forces took possession of the rebel camp, capturing all their wagons, tents and baggage. There were thirty killed and one hundred wounded. We lost eleven killed and thirty wounded. The wounded were mostly taken close to the house, on account of having them close to the water. The rebel colonel died before night. We had our ten thousand troops camped within one mile of the house. Now the tables had turned. We were with our own men again.

I know what my comrade soldiers would say. They would say, "Why did you not go and dig up that money?" No, my dear comrades. I went to General Curtis' headquarters and made a report of everything that happened. He gave me strict orders to keep a guard over everything and not allow anything to be taken from the premises; but the next morning there was not a ham or shoulder in the smoke-house or a chicken on the place, and General Curtis himself told the old gentleman that he had better take care of his money, for it was known that he had it. I want to say that the two girls did nobly. They did all that they could for the Yanks as well as the Rebs. We stayed there until the Yankee army passed, and the young lady never offered to treat us to that nice peach brandy. The morning that we were to go we shook hands all around, bade them goodbye, and as we were standing on the stoop, Jim spoke:

"We are about to go and you will probably never see us again, and we would like to have some of that nice peach brandy, but would prefer to have it without arsenic."

The girl turned as white as a sheet and staggered into the house. The old gentleman did not know what ailed the girl, but ordered a negro to bring up a bucket full. We filled our canteens and took a good drink out of the bucket and bade them all goodbye again.

We mounted our horses and started on after our men. We

came up to the rear-guard five miles west of Jacksonport. I rode up to headquarters and reported to General Curtis: For the benefit of the reader who does not understand army discipline I want to say that when a soldier or detachment of men was sent out from camp, it did not matter how important or how trifling their mission was, they were expected to go to headquarters and report as soon as they returned. That was to let the officers know what success they had, and also to let them see that they were back again.

At this time the rebel guerrillas were concentrating their forces at Jacksonport, and the picket post was doubled. The next day after I got back to Jacksonport I was ordered to take twenty-five men and go out to the long bridge in the rear of the town and do picket duty. The guard had been fired on during the night before and one of our sentinels killed. So you may depend we kept a sharp lookout for bushwhackers. Just as we had relieved the old guard and they had disappeared around the roads, one of my guards came running in from the brush and said, "There is a lot of young pigs running around out there." We all went out but those who were on post, and through the brush we went and got thirteen of them; went back; built a rousing fire of rails, skinned and washed our pigs, and stuck them on sticks all around the fire. A sentry hollered to us that General Curtis and his staff were coming up the road. We formed a line of the guards and as the old general came riding up we presented arms.

"Are you the sergeant of the guards?"

"Yes, sir," said I.

"Well," said the general, "this is a very important post; now you must be very careful and tear up the planks in the middle of the bridge and pile them up at this end, and if the enemy come up set the bridge on fire. You can pile up all the brush and rails under this end of the bridge and have it fixed so you can fire it in three or four places at once."

Then the old gentleman looked around and saw the pigs in a line around the fire and said: "Hello, what have you here, sergeant?" I was staggered for a moment, but finally blurted out:

"Coons, sir."

The old general drew his sword and stuck it into one of the skins that was close by. He held it up on the point of sword, with the little pig's tail hanging down, and said:

"That beats all the coon skins I ever did see." He tried to keep from laughing and look stern, but couldn't; it was too much for him. As soon as the old general could control himself, he turned to me and said:

"Sergeant, don't catch any more of those kind of coons." He rode off laughing while the whole staff followed suit.

On the 27th of June a large force of rebels made an attack on one of our government trains near Stewart's plantation, and as we were going to the rescue of the train the rebels fired at us. I felt a burning sensation as if a bullet had passed through my head. Everything got dark. I fell from my horse. The bullet came so close that the bridge of my nose was broken and made me totally blind for awhile. My comrades carried me back in an ambulance. The whole of General Curtis' army was on the march for Helena. My head felt as big as a bushel basket, and fever set in; then I was in a very critical condition. On we went through swamps, over miles of corduroy. The burning sun was enough to kill a well man; there was no water only what we could get from the dirty swamps. No wonder the men died at a fearful rate. The enemy had chopped the timber down and filled up all the wells along the road.

Some of the time I was delirious, calling for water all the time. Oh, that long, dreary march through those dirty swamps! We finally got to Helena and I was taken to the hospital, and from there was sent to Jefferson barracks, St. Louis, and lay there until Sept. 20th, when I was discharged and sent home. Just as soon as I got well and strong I re-enlisted in the Ninety-fifth Illinois Infantry. The reason I did not get back to my old regiment was that my brother had just enlisted in the Ninety-fifth, and my brother and I enlisted and joined our regiment at Vicksburg. Nothing happened of any consequence until the spring of '64, then we started from Vicksburg and went on the famous Red

River expedition. I will not go into the particulars of this trip, but sometime in the near future I will write on that subject. However, I will give you a few points on the incidents of March 9th, 1864.

The Ninety-fifth embarked on board a transfer at Vicksburg, and started for the mouth of Red River. General Smith had command of our division and we proceeded up the river. The first place we took was Fort Russey. We captured that stronghold, with three thousand prisoners, arms and equipments. We then went on up the river. There was a good deal of skirmishing all the way. At Pleasant Hill occurred the hardest fought battle of the expedition.

Then commenced the retreat to the Mississippi. We were under constant fire for nineteen days, and arrived at the mouth of Red River on the 21st day of May. This ended the expensive and fruitless attempt to reach the head waters of the Red River.

On the 22nd day of May the Ninety-fifth embarked at the mouth of the river and sailed up the Mississippi as far as Memphis, where we arrived the latter part of May.

Now comes the hardest part of my experience as a soldier. I will give you my experience, also the experience of others as prisoners of war at Andersonville.

CHAPTER 9

# Battle & Capture

It is said that we should forgive and forget; but the man who invented that saying never was in Andersonville prison.

No, my readers, I purpose to tell you just as nearly as one man can tell another how the Union soldiers were treated at Andersonville. I shall begin by my capture, and then take you right along with me through the prison.

About the first of June, 1864, we were ordered out from Memphis to fight the rebel General Forrest, then operating near Guntown, Miss. We met him near that place on the tenth day of June, and here occurred one of the most desperate battles I ever witnessed.

A great many think to this day that we were sold out to the Johnnies; and I must say it looked very much like it, indeed.

Our horses, our ambulances, and our wagons were run up to the front. The field lay in the form of a horse-shoe, with heavy timber and dense brushwood on all sides. The rebels were ambushed on three sides of our regiment; consequently they had a cross-fire on us.

Our colonel was killed in the first fire. I thought for awhile that the whole line of battle would fall. One after another of our captains fell, until all were dead or so badly wounded as to incapacitate them for duty.

Finally one of our lieutenants took charge of the regiment. He had no sooner done so than he was shot through the foot. As he went hobbling off he gave the command to fall back. Well, now, you can bet that we did fall back, and in double-quick time, too.

Now, right here occurred an incident that was laughable, notwithstanding the serious position we were all in. We had a large negro to do our cooking. For some reason or other he had got up toward the front. In his hand he held a camp-kettle, and when the Johnnies first fired he stood paralyzed with fear. Finally he got his right mind, and then you ought to have seen him run. He turned, and giving an unearthly yell, skipped across the battlefield. He did not let go of his kettle, and at every jump he yelled, "I'se going home!"

We all gave leg-bail for security, and got across the field in a lively manner, I tell you.

I made a straight line for a creek, and when I got there I saw a tree had fallen across it, and twelve of our men crossed on it. In the meantime the rebels had captured one of our guns, and turned it on our men who were crossing, and swept every man off into the creek. About this time I made a big jump and landed up to my cartridge box in the water. Again, another shot came booming along and cut a nice path through the canebrake. It did not take me long to take advantage of these paths made by the cannon, and get out of that. The first men that I met were of my own company. We formed a line and held the rebels in check until our cartridges gave out; then commenced one of the most shameful stampedes I ever witnessed. We set fire to the wagons that were near us, and retreated. By this time the sun was very nearly down, so we did not get far before dark.

We travelled all night, and in the morning came to a little town called Ripley. Here we made a halt to allow the stragglers to catch up; and while waiting here the rebel cavalry got ahead of us.

The little squad that I was with stood right in front of a large white house with a bay window in front. A woman stepped to the window with a revolver in her hand and fired into our crowd, killing one of our lieutenants. Some of our men still having their guns loaded turned, and without orders, fired and killed the woman.

Just as we got to the town we found the rebel cavalry waiting for us. We formed and charged. The cavalry opened and let us through, we only losing three men.

By this time I was getting tired. I told my brother I could stand it no longer. He told me to try to keep up, but I knew I could not go much further.

About the middle of the afternoon we stopped to rest. We had been resting only a few minutes when *bang! bang!* went the rebel guns. My brother and I jumped to our feet, took hold of hands started down a steep hill.

"Now," said I, "Go on, for I cannot go any farther; I am played out. You go and try to get through to Memphis, and I will hide here and get away if I can."

So he went on and I went down the hill and crawled under a large tree that had probably blown down. It was not five minutes before the Johnnies were jumping over the very tree I was under. While laying there I saw a big black negro jump up out of the brush with a navy revolver in his hand. He saw that the Johnnies were all around him, and that his only chance was to fight. So he jumped upon a large rock. The rebels told him to surrender, and at the same time began firing at him. The negro was plucky; he raised his revolver, took steady aim, and fired. He killed a Johnnie, and fetched three more before they fetched him. Having killed the poor fellow, they went up to him and ran their bayonets through him time and again.

While this was going on you had better believe I was hugging the ground. I lay so flat and close that had I been a case-knife I could not have been much thinner. Well, I lay there until it was getting dark, then crawled from under the tree and went back up the hill. Right in the middle of the road I found a gun, which, upon examination, proved to be loaded. I bent my own gun around a tree, took up the loaded gun and left the road. I made up my mind that I would go about four miles south and then strike west; by doing this I was bound to strike the Mississippi somewhere south of Memphis.

The country between Guntown and Memphis is all timber land.

Well, I went stumbling over logs, tearing through briar-bushes, and finally struck a swamp. Yes, I struck it suddenly and unexpectedly. I struck my toe against a log and went head-foremost, *casouse* into the mud and water. I floundered around in there until I got completely covered with mud and filth. I finally got clear of the swamp and came to a densely wooded place upon ground a little higher. Here I curled up under a tree and went to sleep. The first thing I heard in the morning was the whippoor-will. I saw by the light in the east that it was getting well on towards daylight.

Knowing which direction was east, I knew that the opposite direction would take me to the Mississippi, and in that direction I took my course. I hadn't gone more than a mile when I struck one of our men. He belonged to the cavalry. As he came up to me I asked him which way he was going. He told me he was going to Memphis. "No," said I; "You are going directly east."

After talking the matter over we started off together. We had not gone fifty yards when we heard the click of guns and "Halt! you Yanks; throw down your guns!" "Come up here!" "Give me that hat!" "Here, I want them boots!" I had a pocket knife and seven dollars and thirty cents in my pockets. My boots were new, and I had made up my mind to wear them if anybody wore them. So when I took them off, I stuck the point of my knife into the toe and ripped them up to the top of the leg. "Now you d——d Yank, I'll fix you for that." He dropped on his knee, took deliberate aim, and just as his finger pressed the trigger, the rebel captain raised the muzzle of his gun and it went off over my head. The captain said, "That man is a prisoner, and whatever you do don't shoot him."

Well, the Johnnies did not want my boots then, but they took my pocket knife and money. I told them I had been in quite a number of battles, and seen a great many men captured, but that I had never known one of our men to take a single thing from them; that if their men were captured without blankets we gave them some. "Keep your damn mouth shut, or I'll plug you yet," said the Johnnie. So I kept it shut, you bet.

The rebel captain had his son with him, a boy about sixteen years old. He came up to me and said, "I'se sorry for you." Well, to tell the truth, I was a sorrowful looking object, covered with mud from head to foot, hungry, tired and in the hands of what I knew to be a cruel enemy. You will perhaps say that I was not much of a soldier when I tell you that I cried. I could not help it. The captain's boy said, "Don't cry, and I will give you a piece of corn bread." I could not help laughing at the simplicity of the child, and it made me feel better.

Well, they started us for the main road, and you can imagine my astonishment when we came at last to the road, and found that the rebels had 1,800 of our men prisoners. They then started us toward the battle ground. We marched till sundown and then went into camp.

# CHAPTER 10

# Busting Out

I thought about my brother, but was too tired and worn out to look him up, so lay down on the ground, without blanket or covering of any sort (for the rebels had taken everything and anything that they could make use of) and went to sleep, and I did not waken until I was aroused by the call to fall in. I had had nothing to eat since I left the battlefield, except the piece of corn bread the captain's boy gave me, and this was the third day.

I was so sore and stiff that it was hard for me to move, and in the march if I did not move fast enough, the Johnnies would prod me with their bayonets. We finally reached the battlefield, and when we got there, the rebels gave each of us a hard tack. Then they got us on a train of cars and started us for Meriden, Miss. Arriving at Meriden, we got off the cars for the evening. You can bet I was glad to stop. When we finally got fixed for what I supposed the evening, we were ordered to form in line, and then the Johnnies went through us again; and what they did not take the first time, they did not leave this time. When they got through with us I went and lay down. I will never forget how good it did feel to stretch out at full length on the ground and rest.

The next morning one of our men asked the guard if he was going to get any rations. "Yes," he answered, "I will give you your rations, you d——d Yank," and deliberately shot the man dead on the spot. In a short time they took us down to the Tombigbee River. From there we went straight through to Andersonville.

When we got within a short distance of that place, we smelt something rather strong. I asked one of the guards what it was. He said, "You will soon find out what it is," and you bet we did.

We were, as I said before, in flat-cars. As we came up to the little station, we could look right over the stockade into the pen. The pen looked then as if it would hold no more. I looked back over the whole train, which carried 1800 men, and wondered how in the world we could all get in there. At this time there were only sixteen acres inclosed by the pen, and it contained about 35,000 men. I little thought that I would get out of Andersonville alive; and oh! how many that marched through the prison gates that day came out on the dead-cart!

The stockade was in the form of a square, and made by placing logs in the ground and forming a fence eighteen feet high. Inside of the main fence was a line of posts set twelve feet from the stockade proper, and joined together with slats about as wide as the hand, thus forming a second fence four feet high which ran parallel to the stockade and all around the pen. This was the dead line. A prisoner that came anywhere near the line was shot by the guards. The guards had little sentry boxes built to the outside, and well up to the side of the stockade; were just high enough to allow the guard's head and shoulders to come above the stockade; these were reached from the outside by means of a ladder.

They took us from the cars and marched us up before Captain Wirz's headquarters. We were formed into line and counted off; were divided into hundreds, and again into squads of twenty-five.

A sergeant was appointed over each department. Captain Wirz came out in front of us and said: "You are a fine looking lot of men. I will fix so you will not want to fight any more.

I will leave the readers to say whether he kept his word. The big gates were now swung back and we marched in. The old prisoners crowded around us and were eager to find out what was going on on the outside, and if there was any chance for an exchange.

On the day of my capture I was a hard looking sight, but it was nothing to what I saw on first going into Andersonville. The ground was white with maggots, and as the men crowded up to me the smell was sickening.

Some of the men had great sores on them that were full of maggots. They had lost all the spirit and energy that makes the man. They were filthy, and the lice could be seen crawling all over them. There were men with their feet, and others with their hands rotting off with the scurvy. Men were lying on all sides dying, while others were dead.

Was this some horrible dream, or was it real? I asked myself. I could hardly believe my own eyes at first. Such a terrible sight but few men in the world have ever seen. I looked around for some place to sit down, but there was nothing but the ground, and even that was out of the question, we were so crowded. So thickly were we packed that I found it difficult to do anything but stand or move as the crowd moved. I felt my head grow light. Finally everything became dark, and I was gone. Yes, I had fainted. How long I lay there I do not know, but when I came to again it was night. It was some time before I could realize where I was, but the groans of my dying comrades brought me to my senses.

The air had become chilly. I went a short distance and fell in with my crowd. We all lay down spoon-fashion. One could not turn unless we all turned. The man at the head of the rank would give the command "right spoon," or "left spoon," and then we would all turn together. The next morning I got up and looked upon one of the most horrible sights I ever saw. Within twenty yards of us three men had died during the night. Some of the men were engaged in carrying the dead to the gate entrance. I saw, without moving from the place where I slept, the bodies of fifty-three men that had died during the night. I brushed the maggots from my clothes, and walked down to the creek to wash. When I got there and had a good view of it, it was hard to tell whether it would make one clean or dirty. The rebel guard was camped above on the creek, and they made it a point, it seems, to throw all their filth into it, and at this time it was all the water we had to drink.

I asked one of the prisoners if they ever gave the men soap. He laughed and wanted to know if he looked like a man that had ever seen soap. Just the looks of him would have convinced the most sceptical mind on that point. I went in, however, rubbed some dirty water on my face, and called it a wash. At 12 o'clock the wagon with the meal came in. When I saw them giving it out I thought we were about to get a good ration, but when they came to divide I found my share to consist of two-thirds of a pint. The meal had been ground with the cob, the same way in which farmers grind it for their hogs today. I drew mine in my two hands, for I had no dish to put it in.

After two hours I got a tin pail from one of the prisoners; but then I had no wood to cook it with. One of the old prisoners came to my relief with a few shavings, and showed me how to use them. He dug a little hole in the ground and set fire to the shavings. After placing the shavings in the hole, he set the pail over the fire, stirred in the meal and made a mush of it. I did not get mine more than half done, but I tell you it was good. I had been without anything to eat for three days. I found that the old prisoners made but one meal a day of their rations. For my part it was hard to see how more could be made. After I had been there about two months, they began to prepare the mush outside and bring it in to us in barrels .

Before going any farther I shall give a complete description of the stockade. When I went in first there were about sixteen acres enclosed. The gates were on the west side, one on each side of the creek, which ran from east to west through the middle of the pen. The land rose abruptly on each side of the creek, forming steep rills. About the centre of the stockade was a regular quagmire, which covered about two acres, and this was one reason why we were so crowded. About this time the weather began to get very hot and the death-rate began to increase. The suffering among the prisoners was such as I hope never to witness again.

The water was fearful, and we begged the rebels to give us tools to dig wells with. We dug wells all over the prison, but could get no water. About this time they enlarged the prison and took in eight more acres. I tell you it was great relief. In and around Andersonville was a forest of pitch pine, so in enlarging the stockade they enclosed part of this timber land which, had been cleared, but they contained a great many stumps and roots, which were made use of for firewood. Still the well digging went on but no water was found. We were exposed to the heat of the sun during the day and at night suffered from cold, for we had no shelter or covering of any sort. Starved for want of food and water, hundreds died daily.

For a long time our men had been trying to get up some plan to make their escape from prison. We had dug a number of tunnels, but old Wirz had always found us out. We finally concluded to start in one of our wells which we had dug about sixty feet without getting water. This well was about seventy-five feet from the stockade; so we went down about eighteen feet and commenced digging a tunnel in under the stockade. Night after night we worked and threw the dirt into the well until we filled it to the place started from. Then we handed the dirt up in part of a blanket, and carried it down and threw it in the mire. This all had to be done at night, for the rebel guards were on the watch, and the least thing that looked suspicious was investigated immediately. So we laboured away, night after night, till we were sure we had passed the stockade and then commenced to dig up toward the surface.

We finally got so near the surface that we could hear the rebels talk and walk; so we concluded to wait until some dark night, and then make the attempt. In three or four days we had our tunnel finished (I shall never forget it) it was a dark, rainy night, and we commenced dropping down into the well, one by one, until there were thirteen of us in the tunnel. I was the

73

second. Having got to the end of the tunnel, we lay there and listened. All being still my comrade began to remove the soil.

"Hark," he said, "the rebels are changing guard."

We remained still for half an hour. Everything having become quiet, our leader stuck his head out of the hole. He crawled out, and I, being behind him, gave him a boost. The next man boosted me, and so on until we were all out except the last man. He was the largest man in the crowd, and in trying to get up through the hole got fast in some way. While we were trying to pull him out he hollered. I tell you there was a commotion among the Johnnies then. They commenced firing, and you could hear them running in every direction. The only thing we could do was to leave him take care of ourselves. Three of us staid together and made for the woods.

Oh, how we did run! Every stump and bush we saw we thought a rebel. I said, "Boys, hold up; I can't stand this any longer." No wonder, for we were so starved that there was nothing left but skin and bones. Being in such a weak condition I was surprised that we had gone so far in so short a time. In a few minutes we struck a swamp, and started to wade along the edge. At the same time we could hear a fearful uproar back among the rebel guards. The noise got fainter and fainter, and at last ceased. It was so dark that you could scarcely see your hand in front of your face.

Where the rest of the men were we didn't know. We kept along the edge of the swamp. Sometimes we were up to our knees in water, sometimes we were up to our armpits. We kept steadily on until daylight. Just about this time we heard the bloodhounds away off in our rear. We pushed on with increased vigour. The sounds came nearer and nearer. When it became broad daylight we could see, in the middle of a swamp, a small island. If we could only get to it, we thought we would be safe, for a time at least. The water was covered with slime, and full of all kinds of reptiles. The deadly water moccasin predominated.

Our only chance was to get to the island; so in we went. We finally got to the island, and found it covered with a dense growth of laurel. We crawled up under the brush and lay down. We could easily see the side from which we came. In a few minutes two very large bloodhounds came out of the timber to the edge of the swamp. They stood as if undecided what to do, but finally set up a kind of howl peculiar to them when disappointed or off the scent. In a few minutes five rebels rode up. The head man turned to the others and said:

"Them damned Yanks are over on that island."

The other said, "If they are there I don't see how we will get them."

One of the Rebs then yelled to us,

"Hey, you Yanks, if you don't come over here I will send the dogs after you, and they will tear you to pieces."

We lay perfectly still. Another of the Rebs said,

"I know them Yanks are over there. Don't you see how the cane is parted where they waded or swam over?"

"I tell you what," said another; "I will get astraddle of a log and take the dogs over there."

As he was getting off his horse we heard firing in the distance and the howls of more dogs. The rebels mounted their horses and started for the place where the firing seemed to be. We then jumped up and went around on the other side of the island, where we found a small shanty that had been built by some runaway negro before the war. One of the men, who had been looking around, came running up and said that there was a dugout hidden in the brush. To get it into the water was the work of a minute. It was badly sun-cracked, and leaked, but held us all. Two of us pushed with sticks while the third baled her out with a gourd which we found in the boat. We pushed her along in this manner the rest of the day, and always managed to keep her under the overhanging trees, where we would not likely be discovered.

It was now getting dark, and the swamp was narrowing down and the banks were getting higher. It looked more like a river than a swamp.

"Hark! what is that? Don't you think it is someone chopping?"

"You bet it am. Pull in and we will see."

We pulled in, and climbing out as carefully as I could so as not to make any noise, I stepped along from tree to tree until I got close up to the chopper. It was a negro chopping wood in front of a cabin. A large negro woman stood in the door, and said to him, "Now, Jake, if you want any supper you want to hurry up and chop dat wood."

I looked around, and seeing no other house I stepped out and said, "Good evening."

"Hello!" said Jake; "who is you?"

"It don't make any difference who I am," said I; "but, Aunty, can I get anything to eat?"

"Why, ob course you can, if dat blamed niggah ebber gets dat wood chopped."

"Is there any white people around here, Aunty?"

"No, honey; dere is no white folks within four miles of us. What's the matter, honey? Is you afraid of the white people?"

"You bet I am. I've just got out of prison."

"You has? Oh, good Lord! Is you a Yank?"

"You bet I am."

Jake then said, "Dat is just what dem sojers was huntin' today wid all dem dogs, down by de cane-brake. Dey said dey had catched four, and de dogs tore dem all to pieces."

"Is you all alone, honey?"

"No, ma'am; there are three of us."

"Well, well! bress the Lord. Fetch 'em here."

I then went back to where the boys were, and told them to pull the boat up and come on. When we got to the shanty, the old woman gave us one look, and clasping her hands in front of her, said,

"Fo' de Lawd's sake; I never seed such hard looking men in my whole life!"

No wonder. Each of us had on part of a shirt. Our pants were in rags. No shoes. No hat. And old Aunty was not much blacker. She gave us something to eat and then we went up into the loft,

76

and lying down were soon asleep. We did not wake up until long after daylight. Hearing old Aunty bustling about I put my head down through the trap door to speak to her. Just then Jake came in and said: "I'se been all around and don't see nobody at all." The old woman then told us that we had better stay three or four days, and then Jake would guide us around the swamp, and by that time they would have given up their search for us. We concluded to accept the kind old Aunty's invitation, for we could not possibly find a more secluded spot if we looked a year for it.

CHAPTER 11

# Prison Hell

Jake was the old woman's son. Before the war they had been sent to the swamp to make cypress shingles, and had cleared an acre of ground and built the little cabin, living there ever since. They were very ignorant, but were true to the northern principles and the Union soldiers. Many was the time that our soldiers were taken in and cared for when they knew that death would be the penalty if they were found harbouring Northern men. They were the friends of the Union soldier, and he knew he could put his life in their hands and be safe. Jake kept watch for us, but we did not venture out. We stayed in the loft most of the time.

On the fourth day of our stay, just about noon, Jake came in very much excited. "Oh!" said he; "De sojers is coming! de sojers is coming! What is we to do?"

"Shut up, you niggah," said old Aunty, "I will talk to dem sojers myself. You niggah, does you hear? You go and chop wood." Jake went to chopping wood. In a few minutes three Rebs rode up.

"Hello! you nig. Seen any Yanks pass this way?"

"Fo' the Lord's sake, massa! Is de Yanks got loose?"

Old Aunty goes to the door and said: "Wot's de matter, massa?"

"Have you seen any Yanks?"

"Is dem Yanks got away? Fo' de Lord's sake; what will become of dis pore niggah? Dem Yanks will kill us all. Oh, dear! Oh,

78

dear!"

"Shut up, you old black cuss, and if you see any Yanks send Jake over to his master's and let them know there. They will send word to us."

"Now you just depend I will, massa."

At this the Rebs rode off. Aunty had saved us. She said she never was so scared in all her born days, and Jake's eyes looked like saucers.

I went down from the loft and told Aunty that we had better be going.

"May the good Lord bress you, honey. I does hope dat you may get back to your own folks. I'se awful 'fraid you won't, 'caus I seed an old cullud woman today who say dat de kentry is jist full of sojers looking for dem Yanks wot's runned away from prison. I have baked some corn bread and bacon for you, and Jake will take you around de swamp.

We started about 12 o'clock that night. Our Aunty came to the door, took each of us by the hand and said: "Goodbye, and may de good Lord bress you and keep you." We all thanked her for her kindness and started out into the night. Jake went ahead and we followed along the edge of the swamp till daylight, when we came onto the main road.

"Now, massa," said Jake, "I'se gone as far as I can go with you. I hope you will git through all right, but if I was you I would lay down till night and then take de main road for de north."

We shook hands all around with Jake and he was gone. We then went a mile from the road and went into a lot of brush and lay there all day. When it became dark we struck for the north. It was a beautiful starlight night, and the road stretched straight ahead of us as far as the eye could reach. We passed a number of plantation houses. While passing one in particular the dogs set up a terrible howling. A man stood in the middle of the road. He said:

"Good evening. Who is yous?"

"We are friends."

"Youans look like Yanks."

"Suppose we are. What of that?"

"Well, I supposed you was. My master and a lot of soldiers are in the house now, and they have got seven dogs. They have been looking for youans all day. I hope you will get away but I'se afraid you will not, for the soldiers are all over the country looking for youans."

We then asked him if he would guide us to the big swamp he told us of. He said he would go a piece with us, and he did go two or three miles, bringing us out near a large swamp. We travelled along the edge of this swamp until daybreak, finding ourselves on a large cotton field, when we made for the woods as fast as we could go. When we got to the timber I told the boys that I was played out, so we made for a big brush pile and crawling under the brush ate our breakfast. We then went to sleep and slept way into the next night.

At daylight we again started north. We went through the woods and came out into a cornfield. Our bread and bacon had given out the night before and we were talking about something to eat, when Jesse said, "Hark!" We stopped and listened. Away off over the fields in the direction we had come we could hear the faint sound of the bloodhounds. We looked at each other for a moment and then started for the timber. When we got there each climbed a tree. We had been in the trees only five minutes when seven large and wonderfully ferocious bloodhounds cleared the fence and made straight for our trees.

I will never forget what fearful beasts they were. The froth was coming from their mouths and their eyes shone like candles in the dark. They came right under the trees and looked up as much as to say, we have got you. They would back off a few yards and then come at the tree with a bound, snapping on the jump; then they would chew the bark of the trees. In half an hour the Rebs came riding up. One of them jumped off his horse and threw the fence down. Then they rode in. There were fifteen in all, and their captain was an old gray-headed man. They rode under our trees, pointed their guns at us and said:

" Come down, you damned Yanks, or we will fill your carcasses full of cold lead."

"Gentlemen," said I, "if you want to shoot, shoot; for I would rather be shot than chawed by them dogs."

One of the Rebs spoke to the captain and said, "Let's make them Yanks come down and see how quick the dogs will get away with them."

"No," replied the captain, "they look as though they had had trouble enough."

Then they quarrelled among themselves. Some wanted to let the dogs at us and others wanted to take us back to prison. Finally the captain came out ahead. They muzzled the dogs and tied them together. Then we surrendered. The captain lived only four miles from where we were captured. So they took us back to his house. We got there about 4 o'clock that afternoon. The old gentleman treated us kindly, giving us something to eat and also presented each with a quilt. We stopped here overnight. We had been gone from Andersonville seven days and only got twenty-five miles away.

The Rebs told us that the man who was caught in the hole had been shot where he stuck. All the others had been torn to pieces by the dogs except one and he had his arm torn off and died a few days later. We started next day for the prison. We travelled all day and camped that evening by the road. At noon the next day we got back to prison. Wirz told the guards they were d— fools for bringing us back and told us we should be thankful to get back alive. After relieving us of our quilts the gates were opened and we were marched into Andersonville again.

We had some praying men at Andersonville. They held nightly prayer meetings, and they prayed for water. They prayed like men that meant business, for we were all dying for the want of it. One day after one of these meetings there occurred one of the most fearful rains I ever saw. It washed the stockade as clean as a hound's tooth. Right between the dead line and the stockade it washed a ditch about two feet deep and a spring of cold water broke out in a stream large enough to fill a four-inch pipe. The spring is there yet, I am told, and to this day is called

Providence Spring. It broke out in the very best place it could for our benefit. The stockade protected it on one side from the rebels and the dead-line on the other side protected it from the prisoners. The fountain head was thus protected. We had good water from that on.

As I said before the Johnnies brought in our mush in barrels. After it was distributed the prisoners would tip the barrels over and go in head first trying to get what was not scraped out. They fought like cats and dogs about who would get in first. All sense of manhood had left them. Starvation had made them little better than brutes. I had often tried to keep my mind off of anything to eat but it was impossible. I would dream at night that I was sitting up to a table loaded with good things, but would always wake up before I got them.

About this time there was a band formed, probably the off-scourings of the city of New York. They called themselves the New York Bummers. They made up their minds to live, even if all the rest died of starvation. They were armed with clubs, and would take the mush away from the weaker ones. If the unfortunate ones were strong enough to resist they knocked them down at once; and even went so far as to kill several that refused to give up to them. We were unable to stand by and permit such outrages, for to a man who lost one ration there, it meant almost certain death. So the western prisoners pitched into these "New York Bummers" and had a regular free fight, the former coming out ahead.

We then took six of the leaders, and, holding a drumhead court-martial, sentenced them to be hanged. We first sent a report through to General Sherman, explaining the matter. He sent back word to string them up. The rebels furnished the necessary timber, we built a scaffold and hanged them. From that time on every man ate his own rations.

There was one very large man, who was the only fat man in the pen, among the six who were to be hanged. When they were swung off the big man broke his rope, and then you should have seen him jump to his feet, strike out right and left with his fists, and lay out fifteen or twenty men, and finally fight his way through the crowd to the creek, but the poor fellow got mired in the mud, and was captured and brought back. He looked up and saw the five swinging to and fro, and said, "I will soon be with you."

Then they adjusted the rope around his neck and swung him off.

Oh, how sad it makes me feel when I get to thinking of the poor fellows that had to die in that horrible slaughter pen. I speak that which I know and testify to that which I have seen and nothing more.

I have seen men go to the privy and pick up beans after they had passed through a man, and eat them. I have seen men lying on the ground calling for mothers, sisters, and brothers. No one to soothe the aching brow or whisper words of comfort, but had to die alone in that dirt and filth.

Captain Wirz got it into his head that we had arms, and were going to make a break for liberty, and on the other hand we heard that the rebels intended to take some of us out to shoot, for the Yankees had been shooting the rebel prisoners, and the rebels were going to retaliate; so one day a rebel sergeant came in and commanded about one hundred of us to fall in to go for wood. You may depend we were not long in doing so, for if there was a happy time at Andersonville it was when we were let out to get wood.

Why, dear readers, I cannot describe to you the happiness which I felt to get out of that prison pen for just one hour. We formed a line and marched out. After they had marched us about half a mile from the pen they formed us in a line, with one Reb in front of each Yank, then old Wirz gave the command to ready, aim. You may be sure my heart came up into my mouth, and for a fact I thought the rebels were going to retaliate; but instead of shooting they searched us, to see if we had any arms concealed. Finding nothing of the kind, they put us back into the prison.

The next day the same sergeant came in and inquired for men by the names of Root and Tyler. Tyler being my name I knew it was me he was after, but having the retaliation in my head you may be sure I kept still; but one of our own men pointed me out. The Johnnie came up to me and said, "You are wanted outside;" and looking around he found Root, and told us both to follow him. Our comrades, supposing we were to be shot, escorted us to the gate and bade us goodbye for the last time, as they thought. The truth of the matter was we were taken out to help bury the dead. As far as I was concerned it did not make much difference to me what I did, for at that time I had the scurvy so bad I could have pulled most any tooth out with my fingers, while some of them fell out themselves.

Well, we were taken before Wirz. "Now," said he, "if youans' won't run away you can stay out here and bury the dead." We took the oath, and were told to go to a small log cabin, where we found twenty of our men who had already been taken out for the same business.

## CHAPTER 12

# A Battle to Live

It did seem nice to get into a house which contained a fireplace and a crane where the kettles hung. One of the men swung the crane out and hung a kettle of beans over the fire. You bet I looked on with interest. One of my comrades noticing me watching the cook said, "You had better be careful how you eat, or you will kill yourself." That night I lay as near the fireplace as possible. The bubble of the bean-pot was music in my ear. I kept quiet until I thought my comrades were asleep, then raising myself in a sitting posture, swung the crane back and took the pot of beans off. With much difficulty I succeeded in finding a spoon; I then sat as close to the kettle as possible, with one leg on each side of it, and went in for dear life. "Hold on, there," said one of my comrades, "do you want to kill yourself? I have been watching you all this time." For a truth I thought I was badly used.

The next day the men concluded to leave me to take care of the cabin, being too weak to be of much service.

The provisions were locked up in a big box, and the men went to work. I swept out the cabin and walked out to see what could be seen. Walking along I saw an old coloured woman and her little boy, hanging out clothes. He was very dirty and ragged. He sat on the bank of the creek throwing crumbs from a good-sized piece of corn bread to the fish. I went up to him and snatched the bread from his hands. He jumped up and ran to his mother crying, "That man has got my bread."

"Never mind, honey; that man must be hungry."

The following day three more men were brought out to bury the dead. Our cook as usual hung up the kettle of beans to cook for breakfast.

Sometime in the night one of the new hands got up and helped himself to beans, and before twelve o'clock the next day he was a dead man. You may be sure I was more careful after that how I ate.

The next day the men took me out to help bury the dead. Upon arriving at the place of burial I was yet so weak that I was of no service. So they set me to bringing water for the men to drink. The way the graves were dug was to dig a ditch six feet wide, about one hundred yards long, and three feet deep. They then laid them as close as possible, without box, coffin, or clothes, for the men inside stripped the dead as fast as they died. Most of the prisoners were destitute of clothes, but it looked hard to see from three to five hundred buried in one day without clothes on.

The prisoners of Andersonville were dying at a terrible rate, especially those who had been longest in rebel hands. The rebels had deliberately planned the murder of the Union prisoners by the slow process of starvation and disease. It was at first slow but sure, and then it was sure and rapid. I have counted three hundred and sixty lifeless skeletons of our boys that had died in one day. You might walk around the prison any hour in the day and see men closing their eyes in death. Diarrhoea and scurvy appeared to be the most fatal diseases.

None can know the horrors of scurvy except those who have had it. Sometimes the cords of the victim would be contracted and the limbs drawn up so that the patient could neither walk, stand, nor lie still. Sometimes it would be confined to the bones, and not make any appearance on the outside. At other times it would be confined to the mouth, and the gums would separate from the teeth and the teeth would drop out. I have seen hundreds of cases of this disease in Andersonville. I have seen many of our prisoners suffering with this disease, actually starving to death, because they could not eat the coarse corn meal furnished by the rebels for the Yankee prisoners.

In the month of June it rained continually for twenty-one days, and it is not strange diseases multiplied and assumed every horrible form; there were thirty-five thousand prisoners during all the rainy time, without shelter, lying out in the storm, day and night.

As I was going to the well for water, the third or fourth day of my stay outside, I met Wirz and two Confederate officers. Wirz said, "What are you doing here?" I told him I was carrying water for the men who were digging graves. "Well," said he, "If you don't get inside of that gate, double quick, I will have a grave dug for you, and prepare you to fill it." You may be sure I went in, and was a prisoner inside again.

About this time Mrs. Wirz took a great liking to one of our little drummer boys. She took him out and dressed him in a nice fitting suit of gray. The boy was only eleven years old, and very handsome. The little fellow put on his suit of gray, and Mrs. Wirz said, "How do you like your clothes?"

"I do not like them at all," replied the boy.

"Why, what is the matter?"

"I do not like the colour."

Mrs. Wirz liked him all the better for the bold spirit he manifested. She then made him a suit of blue, and also a nice red cap, and thenceforth he went by the name of Red Cap.

Red Cap would come in every day or two and tell us what was going on outside. He told us Mrs. Wirz quarrelled with Wirz every day because he did not try to prepare some kind of a shelter for the prisoners. She wished him to let a few of us out at a time to cut timber to make our own shelter with. No, he would not do that. Finally Mrs. Wirz told him if he didn't do something for the relief of the prisoners, she would poison him; "For," said she, "I cannot sleep nights; my dreams are one continued nightmare, and I will stand it no longer." Mrs. Wirz was a true southerner, of the kind called Creole; but for all that she had a great deal of humanity about her. She continued her threats and pleadings, but they were of no avail. She finally did give him a dose of poison. He had been threatened so much that when he did get it he knew what was the matter, and took something to counteract it. After that "Old Wirz" let us out of-tener for wood.

Dr. John C. Bates, who was a kind-hearted and humane rebel surgeon, testified as follows:

When I went there, there were twenty-five hundred sick in the hospital. I judge twenty-five thousand prisoners were crowded together in the stockade. Some had made holes and burrows in the earth. Those under the sheds in the hospital were doing comparatively well. I saw but little shelter excepting what the prisoners' ingenuity had devised. I found them suffering with scurvy, dropsy, di-arrhoea, gangrene, pneumonia, and other diseases. When prisoners died they were laid in wagons head foremost to be carried off. Effluvia from the hospital was very of-fensive.

If by accident my hands were affected, I would not go into the hospital without putting a plaster over the affected part. If persons whose systems were reduced by inanition should perchance stump a toe or scratch a hand, the next report to me was gangrene, so potent was the hospital gangrene. The prisoners were more thickly confined in the stockade than ants and bees. Dogs were kept for hunt-ing the prisoners who escaped.

Fifty *per cent* of those who died might have been saved. I feel safe in saying seventy-five *per cent* might have been saved, if the patients had been properly cared for. The ef-fect of the treatment of prisoners was morally as well as physically injurious. Each lived but for himself, which I suppose was entirely super-induced by their starving con-dition. Seeing the condition of some of them, I remarked to my student, "I cannot resurrect them." I found persons lying dead among the living. Thinking they merely slept, I went to wake them up but found they were taking their everlasting sleep. This was in the hospital, and I judge it was worse in the stockade. There being no dead-house I erected a tent for that purpose. But I soon found that a blanket or quilt had been cut off from the canvas, and as the material readily served for repairs, the dead-house had to be abandoned.

The daily ration was much less in September, October, November and December than it was from the first of January till the twenty-sixth of March, 1865. The men had never had ten ounces of food every twenty-four hours. The scurvy was next to rottenness. Some of the patients could not eat on account of the scurvy; their teeth were loose; they frequently asked me to give them something to eat which would not cause pain. While Doctor Stevenson was medical director he did not manifest any interest in the relief of their necessities; the rations were less than ten ounces in twenty-four hours; some men did actually starve to death on it. There was plenty of wood in the neighbourhood, which might have been cut to answer all demands for shelter and fuel.

This concluded the testimony of Dr. Bates, and considering that he lives in Georgia it need not be said that he testified reluctantly to the truth.

Charles W. Reynolds, of Company B, Ninth Illinois Cavalry, writes his experience:

We reached Andersonville about 2 o'clock p. m. on the first day of April, 1864, We got off the cars in a timbered country with a dry sandy soil. About three quarters of a mile off we could see a large enclosure composed of timber set on end in the ground, with sentry boxes set along the top, and that was the Andersonville prison pen. The old Dutchman, as he was called, Captain Wirz, riding a white horse, came along and escorted us to the prison gate. Here he left us with the guards and himself went inside to learn what part of the prison to assign us to.

While we were waiting outside of the prison gates a lot of Yankee prisoners came from the woods with arms full of fagots that they had been gathering for fuel. At first we thought they were a lot of negroes; but as they came nearer we saw that they were Yankee prisoners. They were as black as negroes, and such downcast, hopeless, haggard and woebegone looking human beings I never saw before. They said they were glad to see us, but would to God it was under better circumstances.

After a while the prison gates were opened for us to pass through. As we entered a sight of horror met our eyes that almost froze our blood and made our hearts stop beating. Before us were skeleton forms that once had been stalwart men, covered with rags and filth and vermin, with hollow cheeks and glowing eyes. Some of the men in the heat and intensity of their feelings exclaimed, 'Is this hell?' Well might Wirz, the old fiend who presided over that rebel slaughtering pen, have written over its gates, 'Let him that enters here leave all hope behind.' It may be that some of the readers of this little book think there is a good deal of exaggeration, but I want to say right here that it is impossible to write or tell the horrors of Andersonville prison so that anybody can understand or realize them.

It was getting along toward fall and the rebels told us there was going to be an exchange. Oh, how my heart did jump. Could it be possible that I was to get back to see my kind old mother, and my wife and little ones who had mourned for me as dead? If I could only write the feelings that overcame me I know you would feel happy for me. It, however, turned out to be false. We also heard that General Sherman was getting close to us and the rebels began to move us out of the way.

The greatest portion was taken to Charleston, North Carolina. There were seven thousand of us left. In a few days they marched the rest of us out and shipped us to Savannah. We arrived there the next day, the hardest looking set of men you ever set eyes on. They marched us from the cars to a new stockade they had prepared for us. As we marched through the city the citizens gathered on each side of the street to see the Yankee prisoners pass. As we marched along some of the citizens said they felt sorry for us, others said we were treated too well. They finally got us to the gate and we were marched in. We were then in hearing of our own guns. This stockade consisted of about ten acres. But after all the citizens gave us more to eat than they did around Andersonville, for they sent in beef and other things that we never got at any other prison.

We did not stay long at Savannah. They took us from there to Thomasville, one hundred miles south of Savannah. On our way from Savannah two of our men made their escape. The guards were stationed on top of the cars and the prisoners were inside. Two of our men made a desperate jump for liberty. We were going at the rate of twenty miles an hour when they made the jump. When they struck the ground they tumbled end over end. The guards blazed away at them. I could see the dirt flying all around them where the bullets struck, and we were gone, and so were they, and I found out since that they got through to our lines all right.

When we arrived at Thomasville our guards marched us back in the woods about three miles. They did not have any stockade at this point, so in order to keep us from making our escape they had a ditch dug all around us. Four more of our men made a break for liberty at this place; three of them got away, the fourth was shot and died in two days afterwards. We stayed at Thomasville two weeks and then our guards marched across the country to a small town called Blackshire. As we were marching through the country the coloured people came out on the road to see the Yankees go by. We were in a deplorable condition, the larger part of the prisoners were almost destitute of clothes, and as we were forced to march along in the cold biting wind, there were a good many of the prisoners died on the road. Most of the men were without shoes. Their feet looked more like big pieces of bloody meat than like human feet. They could easily be tracked by their poor, bleeding feet.

As I said before the coloured people gathered on each side of the road to see the Yankees go by. Seeing an old lady standing close by the road I spoke to her and said: "Aunty, what do you think of us, anyway?"

"Well, mas'er, I'se very sorry for you."

Well, to state the fact, the tears forced themselves to my eyes in spite of all I could do to hear one sympathizing word, even if it was from an old coloured woman.

When we first started from Thomasville one of the guards came up to me and said, 'Yank, I want you to carry this knapsack. I told him I was not able to carry myself. "It don't make no difference to me whether you can carry yourself or not; but you will carry this knapsack as far as you go, or I will blow your brains out." So I was forced to carry his knapsack, which weighed about forty pounds.

Some of the time I thought I would fall, but I managed to keep along until the first day noon, when we made a halt, and the rebel gave me a small piece of meat. "Now," said the Johnnie, "I have given you a good ration, and I hope you will carry my knapsack without grumbling." We started on, but had not gone over five miles when I gave out. I could not go any farther; so down I went my full length on the road. "Get up, you d——d Yank, or I'll run you through with this bayonet." If he had done so it could not have made any difference with me, for I had fainted. A Confederate officer made him take the knapsack, and he put it on another prisoner. I staggered to my feet and went on and on. Oh, would this thing never end!

But finally we did get through to Blackshire, more dead than alive. That was the terminus of the railroad that went through Andersonville. I was glad to get where I could rest. To lie down and stretch out at full length was more delightful than I can decribe. Ah. would this thing never end, or was I doomed to die in rebel hands? I want to say right here that there were seventeen thousand, eight hundred and ninety-six deaths of Union prisoners at Andersonville.

We went into camp about half a mile from the town. The

next morning they marched us through town. The coloured folks came from all sides to see the prisoners and their guards go by, all dressed in their holiday clothes, for this was the day before New Year's. One old coloured woman had a piece of sugar-cane. She was some distance ahead, standing close to the road, watching us go by. Many of the guards made a grab for the piece of cane, but she avoided them every time.

Just as I got opposite her she darted forward and handed me the cane. The rebel guard raised his gun and brought it down over the poor old woman's head, and she fell in the road like one dead. The last I saw of her, her coloured friends were carrying her off. However, I heard the next morning that the woman had died during the night, of the blow she received from the rebel guard. You may be sure I was pleased to get the sugar-cane, and it was a great thing. The cane was very refreshing and nourishing, and I felt very grateful to the poor old coloured woman who lost her life trying to give me something to eat.

They marched us up to the cars. We were put in box-cars. Just as the guards had got us loaded a handsome lady came riding on horseback and began talking very earnestly to one of the Confederate officers. Our guards told us she was pleading with the officer to make us a New Year's present. She finally got the officer's consent, and two large wagons drove up to the cars, and each prisoner got a good half pound of pork, and it was good pork, too. Oh, how thankful we did feel to that good lady for making us that nice present. It is a singular fact, that always during our despondent times there is sure to break through the black clouds a ray of bright sunshine.

We lay in box cars all night, and next morning went through to Andersonville. We arrived there about ten o'clock the same day. On New Year's day, 1865, we were ordered out of the cars. It was a very unpleasant day. The wind was blowing cold from the north, and we huddled up close to keep warm. The rebels were all around us and had fires. We were not in the pen, but just outside.

One of our little drummer boys stepped up to the fire to

warm, when old Wirz came along and ordered him back. The boy started back, but seeing Wirz going away went back to the fire again. Wirz turned, and seeing the boy, drew his revolver and shot him dead. The little fellow fell in the fire. I could not hear what the rebel guards said to Wirz, for the wind was blowing the other way, but this I do know, he took their arms away and put them in irons. They then counted us off and opened the gates, and we marched in. We were prisoners in Andersonville once more.

Well, I must say my hope of getting out was very small; for even if I had been permitted my liberty I could not have walked five miles. There were only about seven thousand of us, altogether; so you see we had plenty of room; in fact it looked almost deserted. I had been used to seeing it crowded. We had no shelter of any kind, so four of us clubbed together and dug a hole seven feet deep, and then widened it out at the bottom so as to accommodate four of us. It was all open at the top, but it kept the cold winds from us.

It finally came my turn to go for wood. There were six of us picked out to go. One of the six was a very sickly man, and could hardly walk, without carrying a load. He could not be persuaded to let some stronger man take his place, so out we went, sick man and all. We went about half a mile from the pen, and every man went to work picking up his wood. Finally, we started for the stockade; but the sick man could not keep up; he had more wood than he could carry. We went as slow as our guards would let us, in order to give him a chance. Just then Wirz came riding along on his old white horse, and seeing the sick man some twenty yards behind, said, "Close up there, close up there, you d——d Yankee."

The sick man tried to hurry up, but stubbed his toe and down he went, wood and all. Wirz sprang from his horse and ran up to the poor sick soldier and kicked him in the stomach with the heel of his big riding boot, and left him a dead man. "That is the way I serve you d——d Yanks when you don't do as I tell you." The rest of us went back to the prison pen, sick at heart.

How was it our government left us there to die? We knew the rebels were anxious for an exchange, and we could not understand why our government would not make the exchange. I know this much about it, if our government had made the exchange the rebels would have had about forty thousand able-bodied men to put in the field, while on the other hand our government would have had that many to put in the hospital. The rebel sergeant came in every day and said, "All you men that will come out and join our army, we will give you good clothes and rations." There were a few that went out, but they went out simply to make their escape. As far as I was concerned, I would have died before I would have put on their gray uniform.

We had no snow, but had cold and heavy rains. One night, just as the guard called out "Twelve o'clock and all is well," our hole in the ground caved in, and we had a terrible time struggling to get out; but we finally got out, and there we sat on the ground, that cold rain beating down on our poor naked bodies. When it did come daylight, we could hardly stand on our feet. One of my poor, comrades died before noon, and another in the afternoon, from the effects of that cold storm; so there were only two of us left.

In about a week from the time our place caved in we were taken out to get wood again. As our little squad marched out, about fifty yards from the stockade I saw a good sized log lying there. It was about eight feet long and two feet in diameter. I saw that the rebel guard was a kind looking old man, and asked him if he would be so kind as to help me get the log inside of the stockade. "Now," said he, "If youans won't try to run away, I will help you." I gave him the desired promise, and he laid down his gun and helped me to roll the log in. That was the second time I had received a kind act from one of the rebel guards. The other time was when the rebel captain gave us three quilts. I got a couple of railroad spikes from one of my comrades, and split the log all up in small strips, and then we fixed our cave up with a good roof, and I must say it was really comfortable.

CHAPTER 13

# Home

One day when the Rebs brought in our meal, an old prisoner managed to steal one of the meal sacks. He stole the sack to make him a shirt. He cut a hole in the bottom for his head, one in each side for his arms. It made the old gentleman quite a shirt. Wirz missed the sack, and refused to issue any more rations till the sack and man were found. He found the man and took him out, and put him in the stocks and left him there all night. In the morning when he went to let him out the man was dead.

In the middle of February the guards told us they didn't think we would have to stay much longer, as the south was about played out. Could it be possible that we were about to get home again, or were they about to move us to another prison, and simply telling us this to keep us from running away? Finally we were ordered out and put on flat cars and sent through to Salem, Alabama. There we were ordered off the cars. As we stepped out on the platform a rebel citizen came up with a stove-pipe hat in his hand. He had it full of Confederate money; and as we passed him he gave each one of us a bill. I got a fifty-dollar bill for mine and I traded it off to an old woman for a sweet potato pie, and thought I had made a big bargain at that.

The guards marched us to a pen they had prepared for us. They opened the gates, and we marched in. Now you could see a big change in the guards and rebel officers. We were used better in every respect. That night the rebel band came up and serenaded us, and finally passed their instruments through to the Yankees, who played Yankee Doodle, Hail Columbia, the Star Spangled Banner, and a good many other pieces. Then they passed the instruments out, and the Johnnies played the Bonnie Blue Flag, and Dixie, and a good many more rebel pieces.

The next morning they marched us out to the depot, and we got on to flat cars again, and were sent through to Jackson, Mississippi, where we were ordered off the cars and formed in-line. The rebel officers said, "You will have to march on foot to Vicksburg," and we had to take an oath not to molest anything on our way. Then the guards were taken off, and only a few rebel officers sent to guide us through to Vicksburg. We were three days in marching through, if I remember right. Finally we came in sight of our flag, on the other side of Black River from us. What a shout went up from our men, I never shall forget it. It did seem as if I could fly. I was going home for sure; there was no doubt now.

As we came up we found a good many ladies that had come down from the north to meet us. They brought us towels, soap, shears, razors, paper and envelopes, and even postage stamps, and our government had sent out new clothes, blankets and tents. Oh, this was a perfect heaven. We washed, cut our hair, and put on our new clothes. The clothing was not issued just as it should have been, but every man helped himself. I got one number seven and one number twelve shoe. By trading around a little, however, I got a pair of twelves; so I was solid. Then I looked around for my comrade, who had slept with me for the past six months, but could not find him. I saw a man standing close by me, laughing, but I did not know it was my comrade I had slept with, until he spoke to me.

It is impossible for me to make you understand the immense change made in us. From dirt and filth and rags, we stepped out clean and well dressed. When I came through to our lines I weighed just one hundred pounds. My average weight is one hundred and ninety. Some of the men were worse off than I. You may be sure, my dear readers, I did feel thankful to God for my deliverance. I had a praying mother away up north, and do feel it was through her prayers, that I got through to our lines once more.

We got some coffee and hard-tack, and pitched our tents about five miles in the rear of Vicksburg. Well, my dear readers, it did seem nice to go into camp in our own lines. I was almost rotten with the scurvy, and so weak that I could hardly walk, and my skin was drawn down over my bones, and it was of a dark blue colour.

Our men died off very rapidly for the first few days. Finally, our doctor had our rations cut down, and the men began to gain. My mind at this time was almost as badly shattered as my body, and didn't become sound till I had been home two years; and the fact of the matter is, I never have become sound in body. I have the scurvy yet; so bad at times that my family cannot sit up and eat at the same table with me; and as far as manual labour is concerned, I am not able to do any. The government allows me four dollars a month pension, which I am very thankful for.

Our camp was on the west side of Black River. After we got in the rear of Vicksburg, we were put on what was called neutral ground, and the rebels had their officers over us. We were not exchanged, but our government made this bargain with the rebels: If they would send us through to our lines, our government would hold us as prisoners of war until they could come to some kind of an understanding. The fact was, the seven thousand that I came through with never were exchanged, but were discharged as prisoners of war. It has been now twenty-two years since the war, and there may be some things that are not correct, but you may depend that everything is as near true as I can remember, in my story.

After we had drawn our clothes and tents and got our tents pitched, and drawn our rations, the first thing done was to write up to Belvidere, Illinois, to my wife and mother, to let them know that I was through to our lines. Oh, what rejoicing there was away up in my northern home. When they first got my letter my wife exclaimed, "Will is alive! Will is alive!"

As I have said, ladies from all over the northern states brought to us books, papers, writing-paper and envelopes. So it seemed like a perfect paradise to what we had seen for a long time. Finally I got a letter from home. I cannot describe to you how happy I did feel to hear from my wife and little ones once more, and from my dear old mother. She wrote they were all well, and so anxious for me to come home. My brother who had left me on the side hill, had been captured, but made his escape. He had died shortly after reaching our lines, and my other brother had died at Nashville hospital. So out of three brothers I was the only one likely to get home.

Every time that we wanted to go outside of our camp we had to go to the rebel colonel and get a pass. One morning I went up to headquarters to get a pass. I wanted to go down to Vicksburg, but could not find a rebel officer in camp. It was the day that Abraham Lincoln was assassinated. Our officers had let the rebel officers know it the moment they had received the news of the assassination. The rebel officers had made a general stampede during the night. They were afraid that when the prisoners of war heard of it they would want to retaliate. I do think that the rebel officers were wise in getting out of camp.

When the news came that Abraham Lincoln was killed there was silence in the camp. Every man you met looked as though he had lost all the friends he ever had. It was days before the men acted like themselves again.

We finally received orders to embark for St. Louis, and at the same time received news that the rebel armies were surrendering on all sides; so we were sure that the war was over. We marched down to Vicksburg to take a steamer for St. Louis. When we got on the levee we found only one boat ready to leave. Our officers then divided us up and put three thousand of us on board the *Henry Ames*, and the balance had to wait for another boat. It was my luck to get on the first boat. I never will forget how happy I did feel when the big wheels began to revolve, and she made out into the broad Mississippi. I was on my way home, sweet home, where I would have a good bed, and sit up to the table and eat with my family once more.

Oh, happy thought! It seemed to me as if the boat only crept along; I wanted to fly; I was sick of war and rumours of war; I did not want any more of it in mine. It was all the officers of the boat could do to keep their prisoners in subjection. They were running from one side of the boat to the other for every trifling thing they saw on the banks of the river. They were free men once more, and were going home; no wonder they were wild.

We finally got to St. Louis. We were then marched up to Benton barracks. When we arrived there we heard that the other prisoners we had left at Vicksburg had embarked on board the steamer *Sultant*, and when just off from Fort Pillow her boilers had exploded, and out of three thousand and five hundred prisoners only three hundred were saved. How hard it did seem for those poor men, after going through the hardships of Andersonville, and almost in sight of their homes, to have to die. I knew that my folks did not know which boat I was on, so I hastened to let them know.

We staid in Camp Benton about three weeks and got paid for rations that we did not eat while prisoners of war, and three months' extra pay. My pay altogether amounted to seventy-six dollars. They then sent us across the Mississippi and we took the cars for Chicago. The citizens all through Illinois heard of our coming and out of every door and window we saw the welcome waves of handkerchiefs and flags; and they had tables set in the open air with everything good you could think of to eat upon them for the prisoners of war. We finally got to Chicago, and then there was a grand scattering of the prisoners. They went in all directions to their homes.

From Chicago I went to Belvidere. My father, mother, wife and little ones live about four miles south of town. There were ten or twelve who belonged in and around Belvidere, and when we got off the train there was a large crowd of citizens there to meet us; and such a cheer as they set up I shall never forget. There was a carriage waiting to take me out home.

As I came in sight of the old farmhouse the feelings that came over me I shall never forget. The carriage stopped; I got out and stepped to the gate; my old mother stood in the door; we gave one another a look and I was in her arms. *"Oh, this is my son, who was lost and is found; who was dead and is alive again."* And surely, if ever the fatted calf was killed it was killed for me. Then, oh, how good it did seem to have my wife and little ones around me once more; and sit up to the table and eat like a Christian.

Now, my kind readers, I will bid you goodbye, and sometime in the near future I will give you the remainder of my recollections of the war.

LEONAUR

# ALSO FROM LEONAUR

**AN APACHE CAMPAIGN IN THE SIERRA MADRE** by *John G. Bourke*—An Account of the Expedition in Pursuit of the Chiricahua Apaches in Arizona, 1883.

**BILLY DIXON & ADOBE WALLS** by *Billy Dixon and Edward Campbell Little*—Scout, Plainsman & Buffalo Hunter, *Life and Adventures of "Billy" Dixon* by Billy Dixon and *The Battle of Adobe Walls* by Edward Campbell Little (*Pearson's Magazine*).

**WITH THE CALIFORNIA COLUMN** by *George H. Petis*—Against Confederates and Hostile Indians During the American Civil War on the South Western Frontier, *The California Column, Frontier Service During the Rebellion* and *Kit Carson's Fight With the Comanche and Kiowa Indians*.

**THRILLING DAYS IN ARMY LIFE** by *George Alexander Forsyth*—Experiences of the Beecher's Island Battle 1868, the Apache Campaign of 1882, and the American Civil War.

**INDIAN FIGHTS AND FIGHTERS** by *Cyrus Townsend Brady*—Indian Fights and Fighters of the American Western Frontier of the 19th Century.

**THE NEZ PERCÉ CAMPAIGN, 1877** by *G. O. Shields & Edmond Stephen Meany*—Two Accounts of Chief Joseph and the Defeat of the Nez Percé, *The Battle of Big Hole* by G. O. Shields and *Chief Joseph, the Nez Percé* by Edmond Stephen Meany.

**CAPTAIN JEFF OF THE TEXAS RANGERS** by *W. J. Maltby*—Fighting Comanche & Kiowa Indians on the South Western Frontier 1863-1874.

**SHERIDAN'S TROOPERS ON THE BORDERS** by *De Benneville Randolph Keim*—The Winter Campaign of the U. S. Army Against the Indian Tribes of the Southern Plains, 1868-9.

**GERONIMO** by *Geronimo*—The Life of the Famous Apache Warrior in His Own Words.

**WILD LIFE IN THE FAR WEST** by *James Hobbs*—The Adventures of a Hunter, Trapper, Guide, Prospector and Soldier.

**THE OLD SANTA FE TRAIL** by *Henry Inman*—The Story of a Great Highway.

**LIFE IN THE FAR WEST** by *George F. Ruxton*—The Experiences of a British Officer in America and Mexico During the 1840's.

**ADVENTURES IN MEXICO AND THE ROCKY MOUNTAINS** by *George F. Ruxton*—Experiences of Mexico and the South West During the 1840's.

www.ingramcontent.com/pod-product-compliance
Lightning Source LLC
Chambersburg PA
CBHW032021090426
42741CB00006B/686